Multiculturalism
and Information and
Communication Technology

Synthesis Lectures on Information Concepts, Retrieval, and Services

Editor

Gary Marchionini, *University of North Carolina, Chapel Hill*

Multiculturalism and Information and Communication Technology
Pnina Fichman and Madelyn R. Sanfilippo
October 2013

The Future of Personal Information Management, Part II: Transforming Technologies to Manage Our Information
William Jones
September 2013

Information Retrieval Models: Foundations and Relationships
Thomas Roelleke
July 2013

Key Issues Regarding Digital Libraries: Evaluation and Integration
Rao Shen, Marcos Andre Goncalves, Edward A. Fox
February 2013

Visual Information Retrieval using Java and LIRE
Mathias Lux, Oge Marques
January 2013

Nuno M. Guimarães, Luís M. Carrico
2009

Understanding User-Web Interactions via Web Analytics
Bernard J. (Jim) Jansen
2009

XML Retrieval
Mounia Lalmas
2009

Faceted Search
Daniel Tunkelang
2009

Introduction to Webometrics: Quantitative Web Research for the Social Sciences
Michael Thelwall
2009

Exploratory Search: Beyond the Query-Response Paradigm
Ryen W. White, Resa A. Roth
2009

New Concepts in Digital Reference
R. David Lankes
2009

Automated Metadata in Multimedia Information Systems: Creation, Refinement,
Use in Surrogates, and Evaluation
Michael G. Christel
2009

© Springer Nature Switzerland AG 2022

Reprint of original edition © Morgan & Claypool 2014

Multiculturalism and Information and Communication Technology
Pnina Fichman and Madelyn R. Sanfilippo

ISBN: 978-3-031-01203-7 print
ISBN: 978-3-031-02331-6 ebook

DOI 10.1007/978-3-031-02331-6

A Publication in the Springer series
SYNTHESIS LECTURES ON INFORMATION CONCEPTS, RETRIEVAL, AND SERVICES #30
Series Editor: Gary Marchionini, University of North Carolina, Chapel Hill

Series ISSN   1947-945X Print   1947-9468 Electronic

Multiculturalism and Information and Communication Technology

Pnina Fichman and Madelyn R. Sanfilippo

Rob Kling Center for Social Informatics, School of Informatics and Computing, Indiana University, Bloomington

SYNTHESIS LECTURES ON INFORMATION CONCEPTS, RETRIEVAL, AND SERVICES #30

ABSTRACT

Research on multiculturalism and information and communication technology (ICT) has been important to understanding recent history, planning for future large-scale initiatives, and understanding unrealized expectations for social and technological change. This interdisciplinary area of research has examined interactions between ICT and culture at the group and society levels. However, there is debate within the literature as to the nature of the relationship between culture and technology. In this synthesis, we suggest that the tensions result from the competing ideologies that drive researchers, allowing us to conceptualize the relationship between culture and ICT under three primary models, each with its own assumptions: 1) Social informatics, 2) Social determinism, and 3) Technological determinism. Social informatics views the relationship to be one of sociotechnical interaction, in which culture and ICTs affect each other mutually and iteratively, rather than linearly; the vast majority of the literature approach the relationships between ICT and culture under the assumptions of social informatics. From a socially deterministic perspective, ICTs are viewed as the dependent variable in the equation, whereas, from a technologically deterministic perspective, ICTs are an independent variable. The issues of multiculturalism and ICTs attracted much scholarly attention and have been explored under a myriad of contexts, with substantial literature on global development, social and political issues, business and public administration as well as education and scholarly collaboration. We synthesize here research in the areas of global development, social and political issues, and business collaboration. Finally we conclude by proposing under explored areas for future research directions.

KEYWORDS

Social informatics, social determinism, technological determinism, multiculturalism, information and communication technology, digital divide, collaboration, global virtual teams, media selection, globalization, international development.

Contents

Acknowledgments

We are indebted to Gary Marchionini from the University of North Carolina at Chapel Hill for his initiative to include this book on multiculturalism and ICT in the Synthesis Lectures on Information Concepts, Retrieval, and Services. Many thanks to the anonymous reviewer, for providing very helpful suggestions, to Dorothy Chulk, for helping us in the early stages of this book, and to John McCurley, for providing valuable editorial comments toward the final stages of this work. Finally, we are thankful for the support of Diane Cerra from Morgan & Claypool.

CHAPTER 1

Introduction

Globalization has historically been tied to technological innovation, and the present era of a networked information society is no different (Barrett, Jarvenpaa, Silva, & Walsham, 2003). Information and communication technologies (ICTs) have provided the infrastructure for multinational businesses (Grachev, 2009), created new cultural connections irrespective of geographic boundaries and distances (Komito, 2011), and allowed an increasingly mobile global population to be connected to their friends, families, and cultures no matter where they are (d'Haenens, 2003), in part because they are shaped by cultures who value connectivity (Gripenberg, Skogseid, Botto, Silli, & Tuuainen, 2004). The issues surrounding multiculturalism and ICTs have attracted much scholarly attention and have been explored under myriad contexts, with substantial literature on education (e.g., Saleh, 2011; Siakas, 2008); global development (e.g., Barrett, Jarvenpaa, Silva, & Walsham, 2003); management, teams, and business (e.g., Lauring & Klitmøller, 2010; Shachaf, 2008); public administration (e.g., Akman, Yazici, Mishra, & Arifoglu, 2005; Falkheimer & Heide, 2009); scholarly collaboration (e.g., Luo & Olson, 2008; Luukkonen, Persson, & Siverton, 1992); and social and political issues (e.g., Halford & Savage, 2010).

Before we begin discussion of these issues, it is important to clearly define "culture," "multiculturalism," and "multicultural interaction." **Culture** is the collective programming of the mind which distinguishes the members of one group or category of people from another (Hofstede, 1991, p. 5); it can be examined at group, organizational, national, and regional levels (Duarte & Snyder, 1999; Hall, 1983; Hofstede, 1991; Schein, 1992; Trompenarrs, & Hampden-Turner, 1998), as well as ethnic, religious, and gendered levels, among others (e.g., Shachaf, 2008), and is subjectively applied and interpreted based on context (Takahashi, Yamagishi, Liu, Wang, Lin, & Yu, 2008). Much of the subsequent discussion focuses on national (or regional) culture.

Multiculturalism refers to groups and societies that include members from multiple cultures; it implies cultural diversity, which includes two or more cultures. Thus, multiculturalism means that relative differences in cultural values exist within the group, and that embedded socio-cultural boundaries among members of the groups exist to create a unique social structure. When it comes to defining what constitutes cultural diversity or how it affects performance, there is little consensus among scholars (Shachaf, 2005). Yet it is agreed that cultural diversity is created in heterogeneous groups, as each member brings his or her own cultural identity and contributes to a unique cultural combination of the particular group (Shachaf, 2008). Thus, cultural diversity involves a setting in which there are relative differences among members when it comes to their cultural orientation. Cultural differences do not always manifest into differences in preferences or ICT configuration, yet unexpected differences also occur, as fault lines do not always fall on regional or national boundaries (Takahashi, Yamagishi, Liu, Wang, Lin, & Yu, 2008). Among the most commonly used frameworks in cross-cultural research in information systems, by far, is Hofstede's (1991) cultural dimensions (Mayers & Tan, 2002). Hofstede's (1991) framework is one of four commonly used approaches to understand cultural diversity through cultural dimensions; other scholars, such as Kluckhohn and Strodbeck (1961), Hall (1976, 1983), Trompenaars and Hampden-Turner (1998), provide their own dimensional frameworks. By approaching it as a pattern that is composed of a combination of dimensions, this approach is one way in which scholars try to understand the nature of cultural differences (Straub, Loch, Evaristo, Karahanna & Srite, 2002). According to this approach, each combination is unique to a culture, and no one dimension can capture its complexity, although some scholars suggest that each dimension can be separately examined. In our synthesis we hold the view that culture is not merely a contextual variable.

Multicultural interactions occur among heterogeneous group members and can be intercultural, ethnocentric, inverted, and integrative (Palaiologou, 2009). Intercultural exchanges in culturally diverse settings are the most equitable of exchanges, such that learning occurs through give-and-take on the part of cultural preferences among participants. Integrative multiculturalism acknowledges minority perspectives without challenging the dominant cultural preferences of those in positions of power (Palaiologou, 2009). Inverted approaches are the reverse of integrative in that specific minority cultural preferences are catered to without acknowledgment of a majority or other diverse factions. Ethnocentric (or mono-cultural) approaches deny diversity and assume the parameters of the culture of those in power, e.g., leaders or managers (Palaiologou, 2009).

Research on multiculturalism and ICT has been important for understanding recent history (e.g., Hampton, Lee, & Her, 2011), planning for future large-scale initiatives (e.g., Mahdjoubi & Moobela, 2008; Naor, Liderman, & Schroeder, 2010), and understanding unrealized expectations for social and technological change (Gebremichael & Jackson, 2006). However, there is clearly fragmentation within this area of research, such as has been documented between national cultures and organizational cultures (Leidner & Kayworth, 2006). We see that there is debate within the literature as to the nature of the relationship between culture and technology. The tensions result from the competing ideologies that drive researchers: 1) social determinism, 2) technological determinism, and 3) social informatics. **Social determinism** asserts that ICTs are entirely social products without influence of their own, at times conceptualizing ICTs as tools, which implies that all social and organizational changes associated with technology are caused by social forces (e.g., Grint & Woolgar, 1997). **Technological determinism** presents ICTs as independent and capable of producing social change, which implies that technologies have specific characteristics independent of the context in which they were developed or used (e.g., Bimber, 1990; Pfeffer & Leblebici, 1977). **Social informatics** asserts that change is context-dependent and that cultural and technological forces mutually and reciprocally impact one another to produce change or particular outcomes (Kling, 1998).

Thus, we conceptualize the relationship between culture and technology under three primary models, each with its own assumptions. From a socially deterministic perspective, ICTs are viewed as the dependent variable in the equation, whereas, from a technologically deterministic perspective, ICTs are an independent variable. Social informatics views the relationship to be one of sociotechnical interaction, in which culture and ICTs affect each other mutually and iteratively, rather than linearly. Within each of these three approaches, the relationship between ICT and culture has been examined at two levels of analysis: society, or macro-level analysis, and groups or teams at the micro-level.

We discuss the relationship between ICT and culture under each of the three models. Because most of the research falls under the social informatics model, which emphasizes bi-directional impacts, we begin our review there. The other two models have attracted scholarly attention almost equally, but we first discuss the socially deterministic perspective, as a little more attention has been given to it in the literature than to the technologically deterministic perspective. We conclude the synthesis by proposing an agenda for future research.

CHAPTER 2

Social Informatics Approach to Multiculturalism and ICT: Bidirectional Impacts

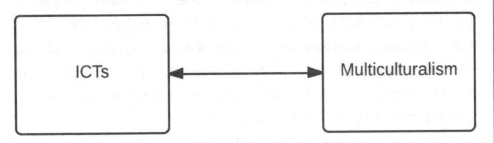

Figure 2.1: Social informatics approach to the relationships between multiculturalism and ICTs: Bidirectional impacts.

It is not surprising that the vast majority of the literature has focused on the relationships between ICT and culture under the assumptions of social informatics (Figure 2.1). Both culture and technology appear as contextual variables in many business models, and social informatics research has consistently supported the claim that context matters, since its inception in the late 1980s (Sanfilippo & Fichman, forthcoming). Empirical evidence of influence in both directions between culture and ICTs, as variables, suggests that impact is bidirectional. Further, a large body of research supports this premise (Diamant, Fussell, & Lo, 2009; d'Haenens, 2003; Easterby-Smith & Malina, 1999; Falkheimer & Heide, 2009; Gibson & Gibbs, 2006; Gudykunst, Matsumoto, Ting-Toomey, Nishida, Kim, & Heyman, 1996; Massey, Hung, Montoya-Weiss, & Ramesh, 2001; Nurmi, Bosch-Sijtsema, Sivunen, & Fruchter, 2009; Pauleen & Yoong, 2001; Quinones, Fussell, Soibelman, & Akinci, 2009; Setlock, Fussell, & Neuwirth, 2004; Shachaf, 2008; Sieck & Mueller, 2009; Takahashi, Yamagishi, Liu, Wang, Lin, & Yu, 2008). As culture influences ICTs, so too do ICTs influence culture, creating reciprocal feedback and interaction between these variables (Dawes, Gharawi, & Burke, 2012; Halford & Savage, 2010; Hamada, 2004; Naor, Liderman, & Schroeder, 2010; Oyedemi, 2009; Schadewitz & Zakaria, 2009; Siakas, 2008; Srinivasan, 2013; Zheng & Walsham, 2008). Various scholars provide a more nuanced model for research that extends beyond the deterministic approaches, a conclusion they have reached after they synthesized the results of deterministic research (Barrett, Jarvenpaa, Silva, & Walsham, 2003; Boast, Bravo, & Srinivasan, 2007; Cozzens, 2012; Gebremichael & Jackson, 2006; Kaye & Little, 2000; Leidner & Kayworth, 2006; Lievrouw, 1998; Mutula, 2005; Olson & Olson, 2003/2004; Palaiologou, 2009; Papaioannou, 2011; Sassi, 2005). Others, after examining each variable and relationship in isolation, have also produced a bidirectional model between culture or multiculturalism and ICT (Diamant, Fussell, & Lo, 2009; Setlock, Fussell, & Neuwirth, 2004; Wang, Fussell, & Setlock, 2009).

This section synthesizes literature that assumes bidirectional impacts between ICT and multiculturalism. We identify two types of relationships: the bidirectional impacts of ICT and culture, and the joint impacts of ICT and culture on successful collaboration. The former are described in Section 2.1 and detail three specific patterns: 1) Mutual shaping, discussed in Section 2.1.1; 2) Cyclical interaction, explained in Section 2.1.2; and 3) Mediated mutual interactions, examined in Section 2.1.3. Section 2.1 and its subsections largely synthesize concepts and present models based on evidence at the society level, as well as a few examples of computer-mediated group collaboration, whereas Section 2.2 primarily describes the joint impacts of multiculturalism and ICT on collaborations within groups and teams, with fewer references to the macro-level.

2.1   THE BIDIRECTIONAL INTERACTION BETWEEN ICT AND CULTURE

In an age of globalization, enabled and connected by ICT, social and cultural diversity and identity are important for cohesion. An understanding of the ways in which these concepts interact can facilitate sound decision-making and better planning for the future (Cozzens, 2012). Scholars have sought to understand both how culture impacts ICT and how ICT impacts culture based not only on the reasonable presumption that there is a relationship between these variables (Boast, Bravo, & Srinivasan, 2007; Gibson & Gibbs, 2006), but also on the observation that cultural, social, and technical inequalities overlap in populations in which they are distributed (Sassi, 2005).

Culture and ICT interact bi-directionally, with ICTs facilitating globalization and multicultural interactions, while cultural diversity affects ICT development, implementation, and applications (Barrett, Jarvenpaa, Silva, & Walsham, 2003). More fundamentally, Palaiologou (2009) argues that ICTs cannot be separated from the context in which they were produced; as products of their contexts, ICTs can further impact those contexts over time. Yet, ICTs are context-sensitive because they are configurable, while culture is not (Siakas, 2008). By configurable, it is meant that a particular ICT can be adapted, re-organized, and controlled so as to conform to intended use constraints and preferences, which are often culturally oriented; cultural fit for technology and cultural, technological congruence are important for controlled change in society and within organizations (Leidner & Kayworth, 2006). These strong ties begin to explain why social inequalities overlap with cultural boundaries and different levels of ICT access (Sassi, 2005). Economic development is sometimes dysfunctional or even conflictual as a result of ICT-supported multicultural interactions because exclusion occurs (Kaye & Little, 2000; Leidner & Kayworth, 2006). Patterns of dysfunction and economic inequality are both outcomes of social or cultural inequalities and of the relationship between culture and ICTs; there are winners and losers during technological change and these changes often benefit the status quo. Both of these precepts have long been asserted by empirical social informatics research (Sanfilippo & Fichman, forthcoming); social informatics emphasizes that despite the optimistic and simple predictions of technological determinists, there were consequences at the expense of certain individuals and social groups, who were different from and less powerful than decision makers (Kling, 1999). Power inequalities map onto cultural interaction with ICT (e.g., Cozzens, 2012; Srinivasan, 2013), implying that inequalities cannot be resolved through purely social or purely technical solutions, but rather require a sociotechnical approach.

As culture, represented by the values that manifest in preferences and choices, interacts with technology, there is conflict as represented through a tri-partite model of interaction (Leidner & Kayworth, 2006). Technology values, cultural values of users, and embedded values in specific technologies lead to con-tribution, vision, and system conflicts in ICT-supported intercultural interactions (Leidner & Kayworth, 2006). This interplay impacts groups and teams in very significant ways, by constraining outcomes and impeding collaboration in absence of, or prior to, the formation of shared norms and values.

The interplay between culture and ICT also has serious implications for global society with respect to cultural conflicts, terrorism, and violence, because these problems have origins in both culture and technology (Hamada, 2004). Analysis of interactions between the Western world and Islamic cultures, for ex-ample, illustrates the complex iterative causation between cultural diversity, cultural openness, and ICTs (Hamada, 2004). This interaction is dynamic and is a subset of a complex system in which culture, politics, interests, distance, organizations, individuals, technologies, and information all interact (e.g., Dawes, Gharawi, & Burke, 2012; Lievrouw, 1998; Nurmi, Bosch-Sijtsema, Sivunen, & Fruchter, 2009). Such complexity is evident, as sociodemographic attributes predict different ICT, media use, and configurations. These configurations and uses predict social mem-bership and achievement; thus, these sociodemographic attributes and ICT use become inseparable and non-linear as each feeds back into the other (d'Haenens, 2003). Similar to the bidirectional impacts of ICT and culture on global society, the reflexivity between culture, multiculturalism, and ICTs is notably evident at the group level, as both technological mediation shapes multicultural interaction and multicultural teams shape their products, embedding in them shared values and compromises (Easterby-Smith & Malina, 1999).

As researchers have sought to understand the interplay between culture and technology, the tendency to argue for unidirectional causation between culture and technology has failed to overcome socioeconomic problems by using too simplistic a predictive model; both technology and culture must be well understood to achieve change. On one hand, technological determinism has not provided a means to bridge the digital divide and provide economic salvation to the developing world, and on the other, cultural determinism has not been able to overcome social and economic boundaries (Gebremichael & Jackson, 2006) in ICT design, policy, implementation, and use. Reconceptualization of the digital divide as digital social inequality allows for more holistic discussion of the shared impact of economics, culture, and technology on social outcomes and distributions (Halford & Savage, 2010).

Digital social inequality shifts focus from the disadvantages symptomatic of the digital divide to the change and stasis in social arrangements that accompany differentiation, exclusion, and bridging of cultures through technology (Halford & Savage, 2010). This revised theoretical construct modifies information poverty theory (Gebremichael & Jackson, 2006), which holds that lack of information or ability to use it is tied to lower economic development. This theory modification illustrates the negative social impact of 1) significant cultural and educational barriers, 2) a lack of access to emerging technology and information infrastructure, and 3) a lack of skills to process or use the information (Halford & Savage, 2010). Specifically, Halford and Savage (2010) found that lack of access created by these barriers led to socioeconomic stagnation and isolation. These conclusions expanded information poverty theory by incorporating 1) actor network theory, as barriers to information access are both created by and limit an agent's social network; 2) feminist theory, as information marginalization is coupled with social marginalization; and 3) Bourdieu's sociological field analysis.

While ICTs have the potential to facilitate an inclusive multicultural public sphere (Papaioannou, 2011), unequal access to ICTs further fragments diverse societies by reinforcing boundaries along cultural, socioeconomic, and demographic lines; reciprocally, cultural differences lead to differences in ICT ownership, access, and use, thereby limiting the potential of technologies to overcome inequalities without complementary policy or social shifts (Falkheimer & Heide, 2009). From a theoretical perspective, these inequalities have been conceptualized along 10 lines: land, labor, institutions, animals, coercion, machines, capital, information, media, and scientific knowledge (Oyedemi, 2009). Particularly important to contextualize cultural and social concerns in relationship to ICTs are institutions, information, and scientific knowledge. Institutions form grounds for inequalities in that they make social, economic, and administrative commitments along cultural boundaries and under the assumption of ICT access and knowledge. Information facilitates informed decision-making and establishes grounds for action, much as scientific knowledge shapes social interventions, such as responses and initiatives within society, both for beneficial and harmful purposes; asymmetrical information and knowledge distributions have significant social impacts both as an externality of interaction between cultural differentiation and ICT distribution, and as an intended outcome from informed decision-making and action-taking.

It is clear that a variety of factors interact with culture and technology to create different outcomes and divergent trends not only in the context of the digital divide (Mutula, 2005) but also in the context of collaborative teamwork (Setlock, Fussell, & Neuwirth, 2004; Wang, Fussell, & Setlock, 2009). Collaboration in global, virtual, and business environments is growing in prevalence and is becoming a central context for the relationship between multiculturalism and ICT (Gibson & Gibbs, 2006; Olson & Olson, 2003/2004; Pauleen & Yoong, 2001; Shachaf, 2008). It is important to consider the complex context of the interaction between ICT and multiculturalism because contextual variables may explain, in part, the reciprocal relationship between technology and culture (Dawes, Gharawi, & Burke, 2012).

In order to better understand and explain the complexity of issues involving multiculturalism and ICT, a variety of theoretical lenses have been employed for analytical structure: Giddens' social theory of structuration, power theory regarding class interactions and international relations, cultural theory regarding networks and institutions (Barrett, Jarvenpaa, Silva, & Walsham, 2003; Halford & Savage, 2010) as well as Sen's capability approach (Zheng & Walsham, 2008). This interaction between multiculturalism and ICT was also the driving force for the development of some theoretical models (e.g., Gebremichael & Jackson,

2006; Kaye & Little, 2000; Shachaf & Hara, 2007). Leidner and Kayworth's (2006) theory of conflict between information technology and culture is a significant example, which has been described as a tripartite model of interaction, and Gebremichael & Jackson's (2006) aforementioned theory of information poverty, conceptualizing socioeconomic inequality, is another example. These inequalities have also been conceptualized as social exclusion in the information society; this is significant because it explicitly addresses both social and technological roots of disparities (Zheng & Walsham, 2008). Another type of conceptual development was the result of overlaying cultural and communication theories with ICTs to better understand multicultural interactions among individuals, in particular within heterogeneous groups (Gudykunst, Matsumoto, Ting-Toomey, Nishida, Kim, & Heyman, 1996; Kaye & Little, 2000; Massey, Hung, Montoya-Weiss, & Ramesh, 2001; Shachaf, 2005).

From a social informatics perspective, as socio-cultural and organizational contexts are perceived to be fundamental forces that shape the design, implementation, and use of ICTs, the interaction between culture and ICTs is a logical progression from the general idea of interaction between social and technical factors. To take Sub-Saharan Africa as an example, cultural differences between the creators of technologies and users in separate places impact implementation and use because preferences and interpretations differ between the two (Mutula, 2005). Simultaneously, ICTs impact users in terms of their limited knowledge of technology and subsequent struggle to interpret intended use consistently with those from other cultures with whom they may want to collaborate (Mutula, 2005). Concurrent impact of culture on ICT design, implementation, and use with the impact of ICT affordances, including usability and reliability, and mediums on multiculturalism feed into one another and are largely determined by context (Mutula, 2005).

2.1.1 MUTUALLY SHAPING

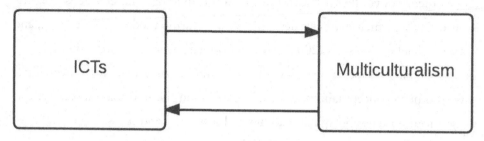

Figure 2.2: ICTs and multiculturalism mutually shaping each other.

It is reasonable to move from evidence that technology and culture impact each other in both directions to a model of feedback and mutual interaction (Figure 2.2) (Diamant, Fussell, & Lo, 2009). Information systems and ICTs support and constrain local cultures and global cultural diversity, changing cultural identity when technologies rigidly impose outside cultural conventions and preserving identity when open-source conventions enable culturally sensitive structuration of ICT (Boast, Bravo, & Srinivasan, 2007).

Empirical evidence of correlations between culture and technology use and ownership illustrate mutually shaping processes (d'Haenens, 2003). Because ICTs serve as cultural bridges, in multicultural settings they are valued by many as mechanisms for engagement, identity preservation, and connection to other cultures with desirable resources or power in their societies (Falkheimer & Heide, 2009). For example, a study of cultural minorities in the Netherlands illustrated that children of immigrants in religious families were more likely to have access to technology and that this access to technology, whether or not the user was religious, led to greater cultural identification with their ancestral culture, with teenagers consuming more media and communicating with more peers in their ancestral home country than in the minority community abroad (d'Haenens, 2003).

Another illustration of mutual shaping occurs as cultural values shape ICT infrastructure, impacting society in such a way as to reinforce distributions that favor cultural norms, rather than to reform or reassess them (Oyedemi, 2009). In this sense, cultural conflict is in part the result of technologies shaped by cultures in conflict (Kaye & Little, 2000). An example of cultural conflict in South Africa concerns access initiatives for the poor and rural minority groups. Failure of the project increased resentment among those who sought to benefit but did not, and increased distance between the affluent and middle classes because the access gap increased (Oyedemi, 2009). Furthermore, social inequality can result from leverage of ICTs through heterotopic communication and cultural values concerning power and control. Accordingly, ICTs can be used to gain socioeconomic advantage, stratify and separate society, perpetuate conflict, and manipulate competition, because they are embedded with social values from a cultural context in which they already occur (Lievrouw, 1998). ICT diffusion initiatives can mask underlying exclusion and deprivations in instances where technology is available but not accessible due to knowledge, resources, or cultural constraints (Zheng & Walsham, 2008). Yet, social justice can be achieved through ICT diffusion (Papaioannou, 2011); for example, in Finland equal access to information, resources, and ICTs within its present economy results in relatively egalitarian socio-cultural structures (Sassi, 2005).

More specifically, cultures shape technologies based on common cultural values, such as expectations of directness, precision, or explicitness in interpersonal communication, and those technologies shape the way individuals with various cultural values interact with each other through technology (Kaye & Little, 2000). Leidner and Kayworth (2006) have compiled a taxonomy of over forty cultural values that impact information system development and use including uncertainty avoidance, power distance, locus of control, sociability, and orientation. Specifically, cultural emphasis on directness, common in low-context[1] or individualist cultures, impacts ICT design and use by providing clear and documented communication. This is in contract to indirect and implicit communication associated with oral speech over the phone or by video chat. Directness, when embedded in technology, shapes multicultural interaction by minimizing cultural differences and personal

---

[1]   Low- and high-context cultures refer to the extent to which communication depends on contextual and nonverbal details in a particular culture; these cultures have very different ICT needs and preferences because they prioritize explicitness versus implicitness differently.

connections because it reduces socialization, thereby creating efficient information exchanges (Kaye & Little, 2000; Shachaf, 2008).

In support of mutual shaping, Dawes, Gharawi, and Burke (2012) argue that both cultural and technical distances, in a particular context, shape multiculturalism. In their view, cultural distance is the degree to which actors from different cultures have commonalities in terms of shared values or common sub-cultures or local cultures, such as organizational cultures. They claim that technical distance is the degree to which available technologies within a given culture coincide with the ICT choices and configurations of another culture. Cultural distance and technical distance have bidirectional impacts, as ICTs are cultural products for cultural endeavors and cultures are bounded, bridged, preserved, and connected through ICTs and other technologies (Dawes, Gharawi, & Burke, 2012). Social differentiation is diminished or exacerbated as a result of the mutual interaction of cultural and technological distinctions and inequalities (Halford & Savage, 2010). In some cases social exclusion occurs under conditions of diminished agency or well-being because of differing levels of access to information channels and technologies central to the economy, which results from the cultural differences between those in power and other segments of the population (Zheng & Walsham, 2008).

Differences between cultures are also subjective and evident at the group level; research on ICT-mediated collaboration between Chinese, Japanese, and Taiwanese students found that the Japanese students felt they could relate to all others equally, while the Chinese and Taiwanese students indicated high in-group affiliation (Takahashi, Yamagishi, Liu, Wang, Lin, & Yu, 2008). These cultural affiliations were conserved in technological choice patterns and the ICT mediation impacted the degree to which collaborators could assess similarity (Takahashi, Yamagishi, Liu, Wang, Lin, & Yu, 2008). Culture and ICTs are strongly interrelated, influencing one another and moderating the relationship with outside variables such as communication tasks in global virtual teams (Massey, Hung, Montoya-Weiss, & Ramesh, 2001).

In contrast to cultural distance and differences, cultural openness shapes inclusive ICTs and ICT platforms by encouraging intercultural interactions and learning, leading to multicultural communities and intercultural understanding (Palaiologou, 2009). However, this openness allows for feedback that presents both negative and positive externalities: on one hand, ICTs enable coordination and transmission of cultural knowledge, which is important for garnering support for leaderless movements, as in the Arab Spring, yet ICTs also enable misrepresentation, which creates chaos and cultural misunderstandings (Srinivasan, 2013).

2.1.2 CYCLICAL INTERACTIONS

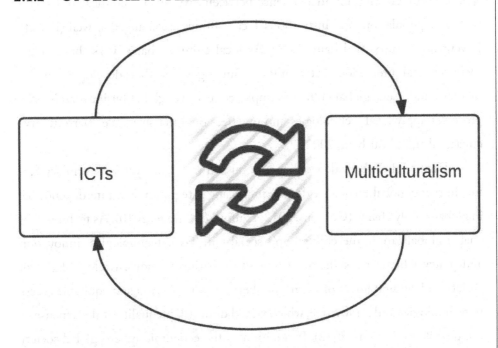

Figure 2.3: Cyclical dynamic between ICTs and multiculturalism.

Culture and ICTs form a dynamic cycle in which forces wax and wane, thereby varying reciprocal impact over time and driving constant change and interaction (Figure 2.3) (Dawes, Gharawi, & Burke, 2012). Global and local cultures take part in this cycle in which they each affect ICT and are impacted by it. It is important to emphasize that the cyclical model implies reciprocal impacts over time, with multiple sequential iterations. These iterations, in which social changes repeatedly follow technological changes and vice versa in a feedback loop, may scale from local culture to global culture and back, or expand impacts into other socio-cultural spheres. The cyclical model differs from the mutual shaping model that implies bidirectional impacts co-occur as both culture and technologies co-evolve; the mutual shaping model does not imply a longitudinal process or multiple iterations. The mutually shaping model presents a sociotechnical change as the result of a sociotechnical force.

As ICTs impact culture on the global level, facilitating multicultural interactions and increasing interdependence between diverse sociopolitical and socio-economic populations and institutions, local cultures are changed as well (Barrett, Jarvenpaa, Silva, & Walsham, 2003). As local cultures shape ICTs through the sociotechnical interactions between the technologies and their developers, implementers, and users, global culture is impacted, because global business and social processes apply local technologies and practices on a massive scale (Barrett, Jarvenpaa, Silva, & Walsham, 2003).

Further, there is evidence that cultural and technical cycles are primary factors in rising global inequality despite increasing integration and interdependence in global supply chains (Cozzens, 2012; Halford & Savage, 2010). As technologies enable globalization, the cultural and social elite favor technological innovation and policy which favors them, thereby exacerbating tensions, while global civil society and cultural forces of the masses better favor cohesion and equitable access to technologies and knowledge, which would diminish inequality at the expense of the powerful (Cozzens, 2012). In addition to the economic sphere, global society experiences inequality between cultural consumers, producers, and those excluded from the global ICT network as a result of social differentiation by information technology (Halford & Savage, 2010).

It is also important to consider that within these complex cycles, cultural changes can take various forms; multiculturalism, intercultural interaction, cultural convergence, and cultural divergence are all phenomena associated with cultural diversity and ICTs (Hamada, 2004). For example within global society, ICT's networking of cultures is perceived, from an Islamic perspective, as strongly shaped by Western cultures that push for convergence, which, for them, is much less desirable than multiculturalism. In this sense there is a feedback loop between cultural hegemony, ICT configuration and potential, and cultural conflict, as cultures that disagree with the prevailing trends oppose potential ICT-driven changes (Hamada, 2004).

While this feedback loop stands in the way of cultural and technological change and reinforces stability and resistance to change, there are also cyclical interactions between ICT and culture that bring about development and support change. For example, culture and ICT feed into one another in a globalized environment as people move more freely across cultural and national boundaries. Those with stronger ethnocultural identities are more likely to depend on ICTs to bridge new lives in new countries with the friends, family, and cultures of their old countries (d'Haenens, 2003). This ICT dependence by migrants, immigrants, and their children reinforces and reforms their ethnocultural identity, which further increases their dependence on ICTs and in some cases leads them to ethnocentric ICT use and media consumption, as well as reconfiguration of technologies to reflect mono-cultural conventions and languages, despite their culturally diverse and multilingual lives (d'Haenens, 2003).

In another effort to show the cyclical interaction between ICT and culture, Papaioannou (2011) synthesized global justice theory and technological diffusion theory to illustrate a feedback loop in which ICTs diffuse further and have greater impact while social empowerment results from technological adoption, which results from empowered groups controlling technology and incentivizing accessibility. In this sense, ICTs are viewed optimistically, but their cultural origins are recognized, as technology and culture feed into one another to achieve justice (Papaioannou, 2011). This argument is somewhat limited by its own optimism, which precludes acknowledgment of the abuse of technology for further social control.

Thus, another important aspect of the cyclical model is the feedback loop. Cultural values and choices embedded within technology knowingly and sometimes intentionally invite strategic manipulation through the feedback loop between culture and ICTs (Lievrouw, 1998). Under a guise of openness, cultural bridging, and collaboration, cultural aspects of technological feedback can promote cultural inequality and conflict and the further control of ICTs by the powerful in order to enable the self-perpetuation of their interests (Lievrouw, 1998). Yet, even in instances where choices are made in an attempt to bridge gaps and integrate marginalized populations, incomplete analysis and lack of understanding of all the variables involved can lead to exacerbation of problems (Oyedemi, 2009). For example, universal access legislation in South Africa failed because the program design did not recognize that those most in need were in areas labeled "not economical," the program had an unrealistically small budget, and the cultural valuation of privatization decreased the oversight of funds, allowing their use to be even less efficient (Oyedemi, 2009).

Finally, this cycle between culture and ICTs can be capitalized upon to improve intercultural collaboration at the group level (Schadewitz & Zakaria, 2009; Shachaf, 2008). For example, understanding what features of ICTs positively impact intercultural interaction allows technologies to be shaped based on social and organizational preferences for multicultural interaction and culturally diverse teams (Diamant, Fussell, & Lo, 2009). Cross-cultural ICT research and intercultural development teams that actively consider the implications of technology on their shared team culture and of their multicultural context on their technological products can better find common ground and manipulate collaboration to achieve desired outcomes (Easterby-Smith & Malina, 1999). Easterby-Smith and Malina (1999) documented the adaptive nature of a team from China and the United Kingdom as they managed relationships and reflected on interactions and cultural conceptualizations, rather than attempting to plan for all unknowns in advance or reassessing at the completion of the project. The team experienced cycles as changes or conflicts occurred and management sought to return the group to the most productive intercultural track. These cyclical interactions affect different facets of culture; in particular, as national culture impacts work, for example in manufacturing industries, the ICTs and technologies used are impacted in ways that shape organizational culture, which in turn manipulates technologies (Naor, Liderman, & Schroeder, 2010).

2.1.3 MEDIATED INTERACTIONS

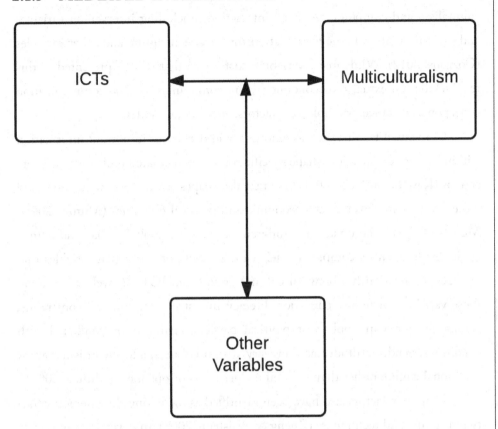

Figure 2.4: Other mediating variables impact the bidirectional relationships between ICTs and multiculturalism.

The relationship between multiculturalism and ICTs is complex and interactions occur across a variety of boundaries. Other mediating variables impact the bidirectional relationships between ICTs and multiculturalism (Figure 2.4). In global virtual teams, for example, social interactions span organizational, departmental, functional language, time, and geographic boundaries (Pauleen & Yoong, 2001; Shachaf & Hara, 2005). Both culture and ICTs mediate the relationship between teamwork and productivity (Gibson & Gibbs, 2006; Shachaf, 2008). Along with geographic distance and organizational structure, cultural differences, technology use, and dependence are elements that shape the outcomes of global virtual team collaboration (Gibson & Gibbs, 2006). In addition to evidence of direct interactions between culture and ICT, various other variables are associated with multiculturalism and computer-mediated interactions, including intervening variables and evidence that ICTs mediate relationships between culture and other variables (Cozzens, 2012). While many variables exist, those that will be presented in this text include contextual and economic factors, communication and communication style, power, distance, psychological factors, and mental models.

Contextual factors, such as emotions and density of important information within a given conversation, shape specific computer-mediated multicultural interactions (Kaye & Little, 2000). Yet context also shapes larger-scale interactions and more complex models for socioeconomic and political outcomes (Mutula, 2005). Models of the digital divide that differentiate between global, social, and democratic divides identify complex models with a variety of contextual variables that mediate the relationship between cultural groups and ICTs, as well as act upon those variables, including education, literacy, infrastructure, financial constraints, communication gaps, policy or political barriers, civil war or conflict, health conditions, gender attitudes as they vary within cultures, and favoritism toward traditional culture rather than cultural inclusiveness or openness (Mutula, 2005).

Economic factors also have been identified as mediating the interaction between culture and technology (Zheng & Walsham, 2008). In developing multicultural societies such as South Africa, economic boundaries often separate cultures, which leads to unequal access to ICTs (Gebremichael & Jackson, 2006). Economic factors mediate intercultural interactions through ICTs at the global level, with the global North and South experiencing and favoring different technologies and their relative economies leading to technologies that favor the preferences of high-wage countries, which exacerbates difference and conflict (Kaye & Little, 2000). Additional mediating variables in the multicultural digital divide include information literacy, or the knowledge and skills necessary to use ICTs, information access between and across social boundaries, and telecommunications infrastructure that supports the use of ICTs, which differs where different cultures live (Gebremichael & Jackson, 2006). Culture and technology are two macro-level concepts. At the micro level, variables, such as self-constructs and individual values, mediate the interaction of culture and ICTs in the lives of individuals (Gudykunst, Matsumoto, Ting-Toomey, Nishida, Kim, & Heyman, 1996).

Communication styles and social interaction patterns—such as inference, indirectness, sensitivity, drama, emotion, openness, precision, silence, dependence, and collectivism/individualism—strongly influence computer-mediated communication and use (Gudykunst, Matsumoto, Ting-Toomey, Nishida, Kim, & Heyman, 1996). Communication styles and culture reciprocally influence one another, with culture mediating the relationships between technology and communication in terms of how a particular ICT can be configured or selected to support specific communicative or collaborative interactions (Massey, Hung, Montoya-Weiss, & Ramesh, 2001; Shachaf & Hara, 2007). Cultural differences, coupled with individual communication styles, shape ICT preferences through valuations on processes for group decision making, problem resolution, opinion sharing, and discussions (Massey, Hung, Montoya-Weiss, & Ramesh, 2001).

Power, as an intangible social force, interacts with culture in a relationship mediated by technology (Cozzens, 2012; Lievrouw, 1998; Nurmi, Bosch-Sijtsema, Sivunen, & Fruchter, 2009; Srinivasan, 2013). Power depends on and is perpetuated by technology, which marshals resources for the control of culture, society, and information. Yet cultures shape the technologies that empower (Cozzens, 2012). Political power specifically interacts with ICTs and culture to the extent that it is wielded to integrate, segregate, or stratify the public by ICT inclusiveness or boundary establishment (Falkheimer & Heide, 2009). Politicians also leverage their power to restrict ICT access, thereby limiting multicultural interaction as well as socioeconomic integration (Hamada, 2004). The mediating impact of power extends beyond human actors in the network, allowing ideas to gain power through mediation of this interaction (Srinivasan, 2013).

Distance, in both cultural and geographic terms, also mediates the relationship between culture and ICTs (Nurmi, Bosch-Sijtsema, Sivunen, & Fruchter, 2009) and is closely associated with power (Nurmi, Bosch-Sijtsema, Sivunen, & Fruchter, 2009). Geographic distance leads to competing lines of authority, low visibility and awareness, and delayed reaction (Nurmi, Bosch-Sijtsema, Sivunen,

& Fruchter, 2009), which is significant in global virtual team performance and integration. Without face-to-face meetings and familiarity with group members due to low physical proximity, distrust, confusion, and inefficiency can take root in practices. Cultural distance, as the differences between individuals based on their cultural preferences and expectations, can be reduced through adaptive leadership behavior and leverage of language skills (Nurmi, Bosch-Sijtsema, Sivunen, & Fruchter, 2009). The concept of cultural distance mediates the relationship between multiculturalism and ICT by differentiating between cultural components within multicultural contexts that interact with ICT, rather than distinctly between ICT and multiculturalism.

Trust and trustworthiness varies across culture; slight differences in trustworthiness impact and are impacted by the ICT environment and culture (Takahashi, Yamagishi, Liu, Wang, Lin, & Yu, 2008). Trust that is a necessary component for team success cannot be taken for granted global virtual teams, as technology and distance may hinder it (Jarvepaa & Leidner, 1999; Shachaf, 2008). In multicultural interactions which are mediated by ICTs, different interpretations of behaviors, based on cultural knowledge or drawn from experiential aspects of the ICT environment, shape users' understanding and trust of other cultures (Takahashi, Yamagishi, Liu, Wang, Lin, & Yu, 2008).

Mental models,[2] particularly of teamwork, intervene when ICTs facilitate multicultural teamwork (Quinones, Fussell, Soibelman, & Akinci, 2009; Sieck & Mueller, 2009). Expectations of tasks, responsibility, and successful outcomes are largely shaped by culture, whereas communication and feedback expectations are shaped by technology (Quinones, Fussell, Soibelman, & Akinci, 2009). Cultural practices and ICT configurations both shape expectations for and beliefs about ideal collaboration practices, which do not conform perfectly to either an individual's culture or technological environment but rather represent a medium that influences both the surrounding culture and future iterations of technology

---

[2]   Mental models refer to the heuristics that individuals use to make judgments and decisions quickly in complex contexts, based on immediate perceptions and interpretation of parts of available information that mesh with existing knowledge structures and beliefs (Gigerenzer & Gaissmaier, 2011).

over time (Sieck & Mueller, 2009). In response to the differences in expectations and configurations of technology, multicultural interactions are shared, fail, or are dominated by one culture (Quinones, Fussell, Soibelman, & Akinci, 2009).

2.2   JOINT IMPACT OF ICT AND CULTURE ON MULTICULTURAL COLLABORATION

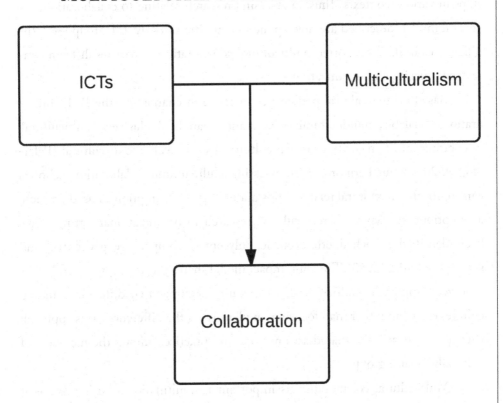

Figure 2.5: Joint impact of ICTs and multiculturalism on collaboration.

Multicultural collaboration depends on technological feasibility and cultural amenability (Cozzens, 2012), making the variables of multiculturalism and ICTs equally important in the equation (Gibson & Gibbs, 2006). Cultures, along with their associated nations, politics, languages, and locations, may shape collaborative technologies, yet they also shape collaboration directly and in concert with their own technological products and the technological products of other cultures (Dawes, Gharawi, & Burke, 2012). This section assesses the concurrent impacts of culture and ICT on collaborative processes and outcomes (Figure 2.5), with evidence supporting all three bidirectional sub-models, as discussed in the previous subsections: mutual shaping (Section 2.1.1; e.g., Massey, Hung, Montoya-Weiss, & Ramesh, 2001), cyclical (Section 2.1.2; e.g., Dawes, Gharawi, & Burke, 2012), and mediated (Section 2.1.3; e.g., Setlock, Fussell, & Neuwirth, 2004) relationships in various contexts. Thus, in assessing research relating to collaboration, the general models described are now applied in specific cases. At the group level, the differences in ICT-supported multicultural collaboration in part result from context, complexity, and organization.

Based on the cultural preferences of those in charge and the ICT configurations available, multicultural collaboration can be inclusively multicultural, integrating into a majority or group culture, or exclusively mono-cultural (Palaiologou, 2009). Furthermore, when assessing multicultural collaboration, scholars can approach intercultural relationships under a set of assumptions. Based on these assumptions, six types of cross-cultural research in organizational settings have been identified: parochial, ethnocentric, polycentric, comparative, geocentric, and synergistic (Adler, 1983). The joint impact model shares the assumptions of Adler's synergetic approach; multicultural collaboration assumes that differences among cultures exist, but rather than focusing on identifying the differences, this approach tries to understand the shared assumptions and practices among the members of culturally diverse groups.

Multicultural collaboration is important to multinational businesses, as it impacts productivity. This collaboration in some instances is shaped by organizational cultures more than by national cultures (Naor, Liderman, & Schroeder, 2010). Consequently, important cultural values impact collaborative teamwork: planning, decision-making, motivation, leadership, argumentation styles, and time use (Olson & Olson, 2003/2004; Shachaf & Hara, 2005) as well as social norms (Quinones, Fussell, Soibelman, & Akinci, 2009; Shachaf & Hara, 2005). In the context of global virtual team collaboration, conflict management (Montoya-Weiss, Massey & Song, 2001), leadership (Kayworth & Leidner, 2001), and trust (Javenpaa & Leidner, 1999) have important impacts on team effectiveness.

Different cultures and different combinations of cultures make different ICT selections, which impacts collaboration and thereby multicultural group outcomes (Schadewitz & Zakaria, 2009). These factors in combination with aspects of ICTs, such as audio versus video, anonymity, decision support systems, speaker identification, and synchronicity at different times of day, allow for trust to overcome distance in virtual collaboration, (Olson & Olson, 2003/2004), leading to more productive collaboration.

Collaboration is often most successful when teams have common cultural ground, shared heritages or history, and ICT configurations that facilitate equal observation and participation for all parties (Easterby-Smith & Malina, 1999). Feasibility depends on cultural boundary crossing, along with other social and geographic boundary crossing, and appropriate ICT channel selection (Pauleen & Yoong, 2001; Shachaf & Hara, 2005), as the transmission of messages and coordination fundamentally underlie collaborative networks (Srinivasan, 2013). Multicultural collaboration is not always successful, because cultural distances can be too great and because ICT affordances and usability are sometimes too limited to facilitate intercultural interactions (Diamant, Fussell, & Lo, 2009). Furthermore, visual and vocal cues, as attributes of particular ICTs, can actually decrease perceived cultural distances and thereby improve collaborative outcomes (Diamant, Fussell, & Lo, 2009).

While the contexts of collaboration in multicultural teams differ, certain parameters of collaboration are relatively universal; for example, team meetings should allow for open discussion and debate of ideas (Sieck & Mueller, 2009). Yet other parameters are not well agreed upon: for example, whether or not it is acceptable for team leaders to make decisions without group input (Sieck & Mueller, 2009). Multiculturalism positively impacts collaboration as multiple cultural perspectives bring diverse knowledge, distributed responsibility, and constructive differences to the team, as enabled by ICTs, to improve decision-making and performance outcomes (Shachaf, 2008). Multiculturalism also poses barriers to team effectiveness through differences in verbal and non-verbal communication styles, as well as explicit language differences. However, ICTs can help overcome these drawbacks to positively aid collaboration (Shachaf, 2008).

In order to understand how culture and ICT impact collaboration, a few experimental studies of multicultural teams have manipulated the media, medium, and culture (Setlock, Fussell, & Neuwirth, 2004); the difference between media and medium is, in this context, that media refers to the communication channel type, such as chat versus email, and medium characterizes the features of a specific channel, such as synchronicity. Findings indicate that culture and media affect collaborative efficiency, with same cultural collaborations and neutral media facilitating mutual understanding (Setlock, Fussell, & Neuwirth, 2004), "neutral media" referring to low-context ICT channels, which provide direct communication with minimal social context, such as instant messaging rather than video chat. Low-context channels refer to those preferred by low-context cultures, as previously discussed. The influence of ICT medium on collaboration is even more complex, with some studies indicating direct impacts on collaborative performance (Falkheimer & Heide, 2009), others indicating mediated impacts (Wang, Fussell, & Setlock, 2009), and still others, despite their expectations, failing to provide clear evidence of impact (Setlock, Fussell, & Neuwirth, 2004). Falkheimer and Heide (2009) found that new media and social media afforded ethnically segregated sub-communities of users easier accessibility and increased trust, making ICT communication in times of crises clearly and directly more usable than broadcast media. In contrast to that straightforward relationship, Wang, Fussell, and Setlock (2009) found that multicultural collaborative performance between Americans and Chinese improved in synchronous text-only chat rooms, when compared with asynchronous or multimodal configurations, which is a more complex and contextual finding. This is interesting when compared with Fussell and Setlock's earlier collaborations, which identified significant impact of culture on performance and marginal impact of medium when randomly assigning same- and inter-cultural pairs to ICTs for reasoning exercises (Setlock, Fussell, & Neuwirth, 2004). ICT use and preference impacts collaboration along cultural lines, with the same cultural groups experiencing less resistance and technological complication than intercultural groups, indicating that culture intercedes within the process (Wang, Fussell, & Setlock, 2009).

Similar to the findings at the group level, at the macro-level both the specific attributes of ICTs and cultures shape cultural interaction and collaboration (Schadewitz & Zakaria, 2009). In order to support marginalized or disenfranchised indigenous cultural groups, preserving their identity and allowing for critical collaboration with outside cultures for the sake of health, welfare, and education, social structure and ICT affordances of flexibility and choice are critical to empowerment (Boast, Bravo, & Srinivasan, 2007). Inequalities and exclusion exist because of gaps in ICT adoption and access, as well as national, cultural, and community differences (Gebremichael & Jackson, 2006; Sassi, 2005). Collaboration succeeds when ICT access can be matched and cultures seek to integrate to accomplish a particular end; collaboration is not viable in all situations, yet is critical to equitably integrating the global community and bridging gaps that leave certain cultures and developing nations to struggle with problems that are dealt with better in other places, such as collaboration for AIDS telemedicine (Gebremichael & Jackson, 2006).

There are also empirically documented examples of positive, successful collaborations. These are clear technological and cultural products, such as global public-private partnerships for global information justice (Papaioannou, 2011) in which valuation of equality and ICT innovation and diffusion yield social equality and inclusion of marginalized populations in the global multicultural society (Papaioannou, 2011). To take an example from the education sector, collaboration throughout the European Union for open and distance learning has been enabled by cultural and technological factors and has in turn impacted them (Siakas, 2008). Study of the attempt to integrate ICT-mediated classrooms highlights the ability to capitalize on Internet and multimedia potential for the sake of high-quality ICT education resources and the development of European intercultural awareness because they value cooperation and exchange (Siakas, 2008). In this sense, cultural openness and ICT attributes and communication modes can be leveraged for desired collaborative outcomes and cultural integration.

ICTs provide particular affordances that make them better suited to bridging cultures, for example, connecting immigrant populations to national cultures than traditional broadcast or print media, because these migrant cultural minorities are more likely to have access to ICT's and social media to connect to their home countries. This is evident in research focusing on Sweden, and is particularly important for providing equal social services in times of crises (Falkheimer & Heide, 2009). Given ICTs important role in this regard, cultural, economic, and social inequality result from cultural competition and unequal access to ICTs (Halford & Savage, 2010; Mutula, 2005); globalization in this sense integrates unequal groups without providing social cohesion, because tensions are exacerbated by technologies which favor particular cultures over others (Cozzens, 2012).

Multicultural collaboration is important because it increases global tolerance through increasing awareness and allowing cultures to interact and coexist, thereby crossing boundaries, rather than converging to a global culture or diverging and becoming isolationist (Hamada, 2004). Furthermore, collaboration and inclusion within diverse countries leads to more equitable outcomes across cultures and through ICTs, yet instances of exclusion and marginalization relate to more fundamental causes in addition to culture and technology (Sassi, 2005). Collaboration and intercultural discourse are complicated; culturally, interaction is believed to be socially positive, helping to diminish differences, yet competitive self-interests shape communication and interaction, as well as commodification of knowledge, which perpetuates social challenges (Lievrouw, 1998).

To sum up, the considerable evidence for the mutually shaping relationship between multiculturalism and ICTs that we presented in Chapter 2 supports the core principles of a social informatics perspective, despite earlier tendencies toward deterministic arguments. Findings from a variety of studies in different domains illustrate that cultures and ICTs do not simply interact linearly; there is feedback over time, allowing cycles to develop in which culture shapes a technology, which in turn impacts the culture from which it originated or an entirely distinct culture. Furthermore, ICTs and multiculturalism shape each other concurrently, with multiple cultures co-producing technologies or ICT configurations and new technologies exerting socio-cultural impacts. An understanding that the model is complex is extremely beneficial for guiding multicultural collaboration in work, research, governance, and social contexts.

The social informatics approach appropriately balances the specifically contextual nature of each interaction and the complex, dynamic, and unexpected outcomes of ICT-supported multicultural collaboration in local and globally distributed configurations. Understanding the complex nature of this bidirectional impact model also explains, in part, why other research has produced empirical support of multicultural impact on ICTs, reviewed in Chapter 3, and, separately, ICT impact on multiculturalism, presented in Chapter 4. The variation in social informatics explanations imply that the empirical evidence for socially and technologically deterministic models is perhaps simply incomplete representations that might otherwise support a social informatics model. These deterministic models, produced earlier and that continue to be supported, perhaps represent either methodological designs that fail to gather longitudinal data, which may reveal mutual interactions over time, or contexts in which either the social or technical force was less evident, though not absent.

CHAPTER 3

Social (Cultural) Deterministic Approach to Multiculturalism and ICTs: ICT as the Dependent Variable

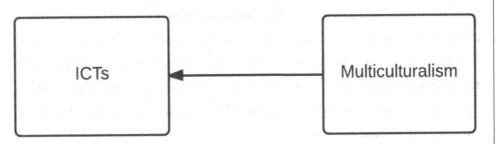

Figure 3.1: Social (cultural) deterministic approach to the relationships between multi-culturalism and ICTs: Multiculturalism impacts ICT.

The body of research indicating unidirectional impacts matches the breadth of scholarship indicating bidirectional relationships between multiculturalism and ICT. Some works discuss the impact of culture on ICT, while others focus on the impact of technology on culture. This section focuses on how cultures shape ICTs (Bird & Osland, 2005/2006; Hung & Nguyen, 2008; James, 2011; Setlock, Fussell, Ji, & Culver, 2009) under a socially deterministic perspective (Figure 3.1). Many studies built on this premise have examined the specific impact of multicultural-ism on technologies (Gibbs, 2009; Lisak & Erez, 2009; Niederman & Tan, 2011), assessing how multicultural interactions impact ICTs in comparison to the impact of single cultures on technology (Brannen, Garcia, & Thomas, 2009; Gripenberg, Skogseid, Botto, Silli, & Tuuainen, 2004; Hsin Hsin, Shuang-Shii, & Shu Han, 2011). Specifically, much attention has been paid to how technologies absorb or are altered by culture and multiculturalism (Kamwendo, 2008; Mikawa, Cunnington, & Gaskins, 2009), as well as to what aspects of culture have had or should have an impact on ICTs (Ardichvili, Maurer, Wei, Wentling, & Stuedemann, 2006; Grachev, 2009; Kayan, Fussell, & Setlock, 2006; Luo & Olson, 2008; Relly & Cuillier, 2010; Shokef & Erez, 2006).

Many empirically documented and analyzed instances can be synthesized to illustrate a larger and very significant point about multiculturalism and ICTs: cultural differences in interaction cannot be eliminated or ignored; nevertheless, they can sometimes be minimized, making the ability of ICTs to bridge differences critical. This is perhaps one of the strongest arguments for a socially deterministic perspective on ICTs and multiculturalism; technology can be intentionally changed, whereas cultural changes are not forcefully affected. Furthermore, it is important to note that from this point of view, social structure and culture shape technology, and ICT cannot overcome or transform social structure (James, 2011); thus, efforts to overcome the digital divide, for example, are constrained by social structure and cultural diversity.

From this socially deterministic perspective, ICTs are tools to bridge cultures and people within teams and across society. The impact of culture on ICT includes impacts on ICT design and use. Of particular interest are the cultural impacts on media choice and technical infrastructure, as well as the cultural values that are embedded in ICT. Section 3.1 introduces and illustrates the major conceptualizations of social shaping of technology in multicultural conditions. More specifically, Section 3.1.1 focuses on cultural impacts on media selection and Section 3.1.2 discusses cultural differences in ICT use. Section 3.1 as a whole identifies and explains cultural impacts on ICT design and use in general, whereas Sections 3.2 and 3.3 illustrate how these cultural forces specifically impact individual ICTs and ICT networks as infrastructure for social interactions, respectively. Specifically, Section 3.2 focuses on the embedded cultural values in ICTs and Section 3.3 presents the cultural origins and parameters of technical infrastructure.

3.1 CULTURAL IMPACTS ON ICT DESIGN AND USE

From a socially deterministic perspective, Bird and Osland (2005/2006) conceptualize the relationship between culture and technology, arguing that dimensions of cultural values of a given individual shape the outcomes and interactions within his or her sphere of influence. In this sense, culture is an important consideration when seeking to determine how, for example, global virtual team members interact through technologically supported means (Gibbs, 2009; Hsin Hsin, Shuang-Shii, & Shu Han, 2011; Shachaf, 2008; Shokef & Erez, 2006). Cultural attributes, and not technology, are directly correlated with outcomes (Setlock, Fussell, Ji, & Culver, 2009). Shachaf and colleagues (Shachaf et al. 2005; 2007; Shachaf, 2008), for example, claim that culture impacts ICT use and media choice, as well as directly and indirectly impacting team processes and outcomes. Similarly, Setlock and colleagues have conducted numerous experimental studies of computer-mediated multicultural communication and have explained variations in media mode and channel selection through dynamic sets of cultural variables, such as uncertainty in social status, cultural identification, or language attainment between specific group members (Setlock, Fussell, Ji, & Culver, 2009). Research comparing multicultural distributed teams with other distributed teams suggests that team outcomes are highly contextual, directly correlated with the cultural attributes of these teams, and not merely shaped by the technology on which they depended (Hsin Hsin, Shuang-Shii, & Shu Han, 2011). More specifically, Hung and Nguyen (2008) found that characteristics of technology in use, such as synchronicity, were actually influenced by degrees of cultural differences in that mutual comprehension in some cases required real time question asking, flipping the direction of variable impact from the authors' original expectations of technology impacting group performance and multiculturalism.

ICT use and design are shaped by cultural values, specifically with respect to environment, time, space, individualism, power, competitiveness, structure, action, thinking, and communication (Bird & Osland, 2005/2006). The impact of culture on ICT ranges from intentional and calculated (Relly & Cuillier, 2010) to unintentional and unconscious (Grachev, 2009). Culture impacts ICT due to intentional control through the imposition of legal limitations and guidelines (Relly & Cuillier, 2010). For example, Access-To-Information (ATI) laws provide stable access to public records and information in democratic regimes, often through ICT-based mechanisms, rather than repository institutions of the past (Relly & Cuillier, 2010). In contrast, there is evidence that Arab culture, which normalizes structural monism and centralization, has been late to bring greater transparency and access to ICT in Arab nations, despite their goals of economic development, which would benefit from ATI laws (Relly & Cuillier, 2010). Grachev (2009) suggests that culture variably impacts ICTs due to subtle differences and innumerable configurations of cultural facets; these facets include saving face, modesty requirements, and competitiveness (Ardichvili, Maurer, Wei, Wentling, & Stuedemann, 2006). Specifically, Ardichvili and colleagues (2006) argue that saving face is an important consideration in many Asian and traditional cultures. For example, in order to ensure that one is not ridiculed or viewed as incompetent, asynchronicity is preferred, so that participants can take their time to be prepared to answer questions or conduct research to improve understanding without having to ask questions and risk looking ignorant (Ardichvili, Maurer, Wei, Wentling, & Stuedemann, 2006). Similarly, cultural expectations of modesty, when coupled with differences in hierarchical cultures, lead to different ICT preferences, uses, and configurations regarding knowledge sharing, knowledge hoarding, and persistence of records. Modesty and collectivism produce records, but also a hesitancy to be recognized for sharing. On the other hand, competitive, individualistic, and hierarchical societies tend to minimize archives, hoard information for personal benefit, and share only when recognition will improve the status of the individual (Ardichvili, Maurer, Wei, Wentling, & Stuedemann, 2006). Facets of culture also manifest specific values, such as power distance and hierarchy or collectivism in social organization, in terms of the behaviors and expectations of members (Ardichvili, Maurer, Wei, Wentling, & Stuedemann, 2006).

Culture also impacts ICTs in terms of their 1) function and design, 2) use, and 3) system implementation. With respect to ICT design and function, those who prioritize information control will design and employ technologies that reinforce their power to control; in contrast, those who prioritize dissemination and multilingual accessibility ensure ICT function empowers those who need the information (Kamwendo, 2008). Furthermore, the global nature of the software and technology sectors greatly impacts ICT design for local and global markets (Gibbs, 2009; Mikawa, Cunnington, & Gaskins, 2009; Niederman & Tan, 2011). More specifically, cultural contexts render identical ICTs in the development stage completely different in use, as is evident in studies of rural development projects in the European Union (Gripenberg, Skogseid, Botto, Silli, & Tuuainen, 2004). Usability of a particular technology is shaped by the cultural values of its creators; for example, emphasis on inclusivity yields lower barriers to entry in terms of cost, learnability, and portability (Kamwendo, 2008). Thus it is clear that ICTs are largely cultural products, as ICTs are created and used by the most affluent, powerful, and educated members of society, and social stratification within and between cultures makes those technologies representative of and controlled by particular cultures and cultural subsets (Luo & Olson, 2008).

With respect to ICT use, user identification of his or her cultural attitudes towards ICTs affects work effectiveness in general, and effectiveness of ICT use in particular. Thus, as technologies are shaped by particular cultures, and the cultural orientation of individuals leads them to feel included or excluded (Brannen, Garcia, & Thomas, 2009), ICT meaning and use are affected by culture accordingly. Different cultures both prioritize ICTs differently and different aspects and configurations of ICTs (Kayan, Fussell, & Setlock, 2006). At the group level effectiveness of ICT use depends on cultural consensus; groups aim to achieve collaborative common ground, because distributed teams with different preferences and relationships to particular technologies cannot function efficiently until shared values and norms are identified and decisions are made for consistency (Shokef & Erez, 2006). Cultural tensions also shape technology, because they integrate and fragment ICTs in use (Gibbs, 2009). Multicultural teams that form a shared culture with unique internal norms and values (Shachaf, 2008) are able to better make technology work for them in support of effective collaboration, whereas groups with cultural barriers find technological mediation of their group to be dysfunctional (Lisak & Erez, 2009).

With respect to successful system implementation, an understanding of how culture impacts technological outcomes is critical (Grachev, 2009). In order to intentionally configure technology in the best way for the organizational, national, or ethnic cultures of users, cultural assessments should be a part of information system development and selection (Ardichvili, Maurer, Wei, Wentling, & Stuedemann, 2006). Furthermore, understanding of particular users is critical to successful ICT implementations, because generalizations and stereotypes are not sufficient to accommodate the reality of multicultural interactions (Bird & Osland, 2005/2006). For example, misunderstanding of bicultural team members' identifications may lead to oversimplification or extraneous complication of technology. This is manifested clearly in a study of Chinese Americans that found that these individuals might identify with their home or ancestral cultures (one-home), with different cultures under different circumstances (either/or), with neither culture (neither/nor), or with both cultures (both/and) (Brannen, Garcia, & Thomas, 2009).

3.1.1   MULTICULTURALISM SHAPES MEDIA SELECTION

Culture impacts media choice in intra- and inter-cultural communication (Ardichvili, Maurer, Wei, Wentling, & Stuedemann, 2006; Hung & Nguyen, 2008; Kamwendo, 2008; Kayan, Fussell, & Setlock, 2006; Massey, Hung, Montoya-Weiss, & Ramesh, 2001; Setlock, Fussell, Ji, & Culver, 2009; Shachaf & Hara, 2007; Shachaf, 2008; Shokef & Erez, 2006). Different ICT modes are preferred in different cultural contexts, because different cultures prioritize different affordances; within a same-culture group, more consistent media choices are made than in multicultural groups, where conflict can occur over the wider variety of media choices (Hung & Nguyen, 2008). The range of channels for effective communication is more limited when communicating with members of other cultures (Shachaf & Hara, 2007). The complexity of relationships within global virtual teams and the nuances of social identity can be mapped onto these choices to explain why cultural diversity shapes multicultural virtual communication environments (Hung & Nguyen, 2008).

For example, in one study, teams comprised of native English-speaking Americans and native Chinese-speaking Chinese members who had never met face-to-face were more likely to select high-context, synchronous modes of communication, such as video chat, or multimodal interactions in order to balance social advantages and maximize social cues than are pairs of bilingual Chinese Americans and Chinese, who share some cultural ground (Hung & Nguyen, 2008). In another study, cultural differences led to different ICT choices for intercultural interaction: although North American, Indian, and East Asian graduate students and young professionals all used IM clients, they selected different clients with different features and used them differently. For example, Indians sent messages to offline contacts at a much higher rate and preferred video chat to other media features, using it more often than students from other cultures, which led them to favor Yahoo over other clients, because they wanted these features. East Asian students enjoyed the social affordances of multiparty chat more than students from other cultures (Kayan, Fussell, & Setlock, 2006). In a third study, other differences in media selection between Asian and North American students resulted from intercultural interactions. Preferences for synchronicity, anonymity, and mode when interacting within culture or across culture varied based on cultural uncertainty, status uncertainty, and language uncertainty (Setlock, Fussell, Ji, & Culver, 2009). Differences in technology use and in the perception of task technology fit among Eastern and Western cultures exist. For instance, Lee (2002) found that patterns of email use vary between Eastern and Western cultures due to their cultural differences. Likewise, Massey et al. (2001) found significant differences in the perception of task technology fit between virtual team members from the U.S., Asia, and Europe. In the workplace, members from various cultural backgrounds preferred a textual media channel for intercultural communication, as it reduces noise and limits miscommunication in global virtual teams (Shachaf, 2008). Shachaf and Hara (2007) developed a behavioral complexity theory for media selection in global virtual teams: as channels fail to meet the needs of a particular multicultural interaction, they are eliminated as potential modes of interaction, based on the criteria of physical and social proximities, tasks, channel accessibility for each collaborator, personal preferences, and channel of origin for the collaboration (Shachaf & Hara, 2007). Thus, for interaction between members of the same culture, a wider range of media can be used effectively, whereas in complex heterogeneous settings, the range is more limited by additional contingencies involved (Shachaf, 2008).

Understanding media selection by culture, in order to better facilitate intercultural interactions, has serious implications for team effectiveness in business. Analysis of a multinational organization with virtual collaboration between offices in Russia, China, and Brazil revealed variation in communication channel selection based on cultural tendencies toward directness of interaction, strictness of hierarchy in their culture, and emphasis on accountability, which would necessitate communication through technologies with paper trails or records, such as email (Ardichvili, Maurer, Wei, Wentling, & Stuedemann, 2006). Specifically, Russians preferred indirect communication through email, as it transcended social boundaries by making communicants distant from one another. Chinese preferred direct, equitable, and highly identifiable communication face-to-face or by audio or visual ICT because they sought to outcompete members of other cultures and distrusted persistent information and sharing. Brazilians were culturally conflicted between preferences for direct, synchronous interaction and the accountability documentation provides; this represents the conflict between their direct, personal culture and the pervasive social problems which have developed due to lack of accountability without communication records (Ardichvili, Maurer, Wei, Wentling, & Stuedemann, 2006). The authors explain these differences in preference by national culture and historical cultural development. For example, the collectivist nature of Chinese culture encouraged high integration with the group, whereas Russian skepticism and desire to get ahead after historical stagnation led to preferences that facilitated working at their own pace (Ardichvili, Maurer, Wei, Wentling, & Stuedemann, 2006). In this context of intercultural interaction, ICTs through which written communication is possible, such as instant messaging or email, are often preferred, so that precise and concise wording can reduce uncertainty (Setlock, Fussell, Ji, & Culver, 2009; Shachaf & Hara, 2007). Reduction of uncertainty and emphasis on directness and focus are logical desires in multicultural interaction, which can easily be met through deliberative ICT selection (Shachaf, 2008).

Multiculturalism shapes ICT channel selection based on the needs of interaction, as well as the differences in cultural preferences. Shokef and Erez (2006) and Kamwendo (2008) illustrate how ICT selection is shaped by culture based largely on the affordances and usability of a given technology. Specific cultural preferences that lead to affinity for particular affordances include competitive orientation, flexibility, tolerance of change and diversity, social responsibility, collectivism, power distance, and uncertainty avoidance (Shokef & Erez, 2006). Needs within particular interactions often require detailed understanding of differences in preferences, including how the needs and preferences of a society may differ from the expectations and preferences of those in power. Kamwendo (2008) studied viability of technologies and communication media selection in Malawi in order to determine how information could actually be disseminated to a population in extreme poverty, with low literacy, and that speaks many different languages. This analysis revealed differences between effectiveness for the population and what would be most efficient for decision-makers. The author determined that broadcast communication through radio within Malawi has been most equitably shaped based on the conception that information was empowering and should be spoken so as to be most comprehensible, rather than ICTs that are expensive and more dependent on literacy.

3.1.2 MEMBERS OF DIFFERENT CULTURES USE ICTS DIFFERENTLY

In different cultural contexts, ICTs are used and understood in completely different ways (Gripenberg, Skogseid, Botto, Silli, & Tuuainen, 2004). For example, majority cultures, powerful cultures, and Westernized cultures have different technological needs and abilities. Government officials and bureaucrats often fail in designing ICT development initiatives for rural and traditional cultures, because they mistakenly assume that ICTs are transformative in realizing social change (Gripenberg, Skogseid, Botto, Silli, & Tuuainen, 2004). However, ICTs do not uniformly impart themselves on cultures, but rather cultural groups adapt them to the extent possible or desired to meet their local needs (Gripenberg, Skogseid, Botto, Silli, & Tuuainen, 2004).

Some differences in ICT use are the result of complex intercultural interactions and social structures. Specifically, the use of technology within the developed world is ubiquitous and implicit in the high performing networks that scholarly, government, and corporate scientists form. In contrast, ICT use within the developing world represents careful and deliberate choices to connect only the most helpful points to outside developed networks, so as to meet their most urgent public needs (Luo & Olson, 2008). Cultural divides between developed and developing nations and regions yield technological differences, just as economic divides do. These cultural differences, coupled with economic inequality, lead to different values and decisions regarding technological investment and use. ICTs are not very accessible and infrastructure is insufficient for all demands, yet ICT investment is prioritized for particular purposes, such as information sharing for treatment and control of the AIDS epidemic in developing nations, representing value choices based on the most pressing cultural needs (Luo & Olson, 2008).

When members of multiple cultures interact in groups or dyads, ICT performance is often inefficient, because preferences and practices differ. Multicultural interactions that depend on ICT for communicative or collaborative purposes are complicated, because use of one ICT does not guarantee consistency in ICT practice by all members. Communication quality and performance vary drastically based on the levels of cultural adaptation, similarity, and trust within global virtual teams.

It is evident that group composition has both direct and mediated impacts on group outcomes in traditional groups that do not use ICT (Early & Mosakowski, 2000; Oetzel, 2001). Early and Mosakowski (2000), for instance, found that highly heterogeneous teams and highly homogeneous teams exhibit high levels of productivity, while moderately heterogeneous teams have lower levels of productivity. Other studies, including those that involved computer mediated groups, which compare heterogeneous and homogeneous teams, conclude that diversity increases effectiveness (Daily & Steiner, 1998; Daily, Whatley, Ash & Steiner, 1996). Multiculturalism enables increases in performance and creativity, due to a wider range of perspectives, more and better ideas, and less groupthink. Daily and Steiner (1998) found that computer mediated heterogeneous teams were more creative and more innovative. When heterogeneous teams used group-decision support systems, they outperformed heterogeneous groups that did not use technology (Daily & Steiner, 1998; Daily et al., 1996). Still, ICT mediated heterogeneous teams, compared with homogeneous teams, faced additional communication barriers as multiculturalism increases the complexity, conflict, confusion, and ambiguity of communication and may decrease virtual team performance (Daily & Steiner, 1998; Shachaf, 2008).

As groups coalesce into their own inclusive, hybrid culture, efficiency and productivity increases as perceived difference diminishes and cultural barriers to communication are reduced (Hsin Hsin, Shuang-Shii, & Shu Han, 2011). Furthermore, global virtual teams experience different communication quality and technological mediation based on leaders' culture and teams' cultural identities, thereby leading to differences in performance levels based on cultural differences in ICT use habits. Performance levels of culturally heterogeneous groups vary because they use technology differently without establishing a shared team culture or common practice (Lisak & Erez, 2009). Specifically, Lisak and Erez sought to understand the impact of transformational leadership on multicultural teams and found that, rather than clearly impacting performance, performance was influenced most positively by development of a shared multicultural identity and selection of common ICT use standards. Leadership alone could not overcome the inefficiencies of many culturally affiliated use patterns of ICTs on the collaborative project (Lisak & Erez, 2009). Research into the effects of virtual team composition on performance suggests that composition impacts team performance in the virtual environment (Wong & Burton, 2000). However, research about the influence of heterogeneous composition on team effectiveness in FTF teams leads to mixed findings (Guzzo & Dickson, 1996). Still, it is important to understand the effect of cultural diversity on global virtual team effectiveness (Cohen & Bailey, 1997; Jarvenpaa & Leidner 1999; Dafoulas & Macaulay, 2001; Shachaf, 2008).

Differences in ICT use by different cultural groups affect more than productivity and efficiency; these differences also impact shared knowledge, communication, and learning within organizations. At Caterpillar, for example, ICTs that were designed to facilitate knowledge management and diffusion among offices in multiple countries revealed significant differences in the use of ICTs and effectiveness of knowledge management systems, including differences by ethnic cultural identities in contributions and participation, mediation of interaction, and documentation of queries (Ardichvili, Maurer, Wei, Wentling, & Stuedemann, 2006). Individuals from Eastern and Western cultures have been shown to use technologies differently in less formal contexts as well, with individuals from Western cultures preferring one-to-one communication with minimal excess features, while individuals from Eastern cultures preferred to use multi-modal ICTs as virtual spaces for many collaborators (Kayan, Fussell, & Setlock, 2006). While these differences may appear not to change the technologies fundamentally, but rather to capitalize on different functions in multicultural interactions, there is significant cultural impact on the affordances, meaning, and usability of technologies (Ardichvili, Maurer, Wei, Wentling, & Stuedemann, 2006; Kayan, Fussell, & Setlock, 2006), as well as implications for future technological development to support multicultural interactions through modal and functional options.

3.2   EMBEDDED CULTURAL VALUES IN ICTS

Cultures embed their values within ICTs as choices are made with respect to technological development and configuration. Through the identification and analysis of cultural expectations, ICTs are designed to suit specific cultural contexts, whether multicultural or ethnocentric, and sometimes reflect majority or dominant cultural values over inclusivity, whether that is intentional or not (Bird & Osland, 2005/2006). Technologies are cultural products; when social inequality underlies the production of technology, and social inequality drives the distribution of technologies, technologies cannot be expected to escape the values embedded within them (James, 2011). When different cultural value sets come into contact, technologies that represent a particular set of values can exacerbate social conflict and differentiation (Fleischmann, 2007).

Cultures impact both ICT design and use, based on fundamental and shared social values (Fleishmann, forthcoming). Values are embedded in use when certain features are avoided or routinely used in order to satisfy cultural values such as transparency (Relly & Cuillier, 2010) or accountability (Ardichvili, Maurer, Wei, Wentling, & Stuedemann, 2006), as Section 3.1.2 discussed. Additionally, values are embedded in design when developers make choices based on their own cultural preferences or as a result of compromise following value conflict within multicultural teams (Fleischmann, Wallace, & Grimes, 2011). These processes and the distinction between use and design are complex and the subject of an extensive body of research, as is outlined, for example, by Fleischmann (forthcoming), but is beyond our scope; we only briefly refer to this area of research as related to multiculturalism.

From a global perspective, ICT production is emblematic of other multinational industries and specific products and technologies are produced in multicultural environments under corporate strategies. The economic imperative underlying these strategies, shaped by political and cultural imperatives, distributes and configures stages of design, production, and distribution in different national cultural contexts, leading to contextual decision-making about these technologies (Grachev, 2009; Mikawa, Cunnington, & Gaskins, 2009). From a humanistic perspective, ICT distribution also follows the distribution patterns of other significant goods. The affluent have access to ICTs and value ICT as useful for educational, business, and social endeavors, and therefore seek to increase accessibility but only recognize inaccessibility from afar, rather than the inequality within their own countries (James, 2011).

At the group level, ICT production and configuration is shaped by the cultural preferences of the designers (Fleischmann, Wallace, & Grimes, 2011). Individualistic and collectivistic cultures lead to variations in ICT design and use.

For example, cultural differences between members of global virtual IT teams lead to necessary value choices, as cultural preferences compete and thereby impact ICT development. To take a specific example, as team members differ in individualism and collectivism, and disagree over challenge and compensation, tradeoffs are made which lead to value choices about standards, labels, anonymity, explicitness, and embeddedness (Niederman & Tan, 2011). Specifically, agreement on standards and labels will ensure that team members speak the same language and have the same constructs in mind in their work, rather than sub-groups working with different concepts. Cultural preference for anonymous contributions within a group, so as to recognize group achievements versus individual achievements, are significant differences for which expectations must be made clear so as to create consistency. The need for clarity for productive group work is also where the issue of explicitness must be reconciled with the preference in some cultures not to commit to precise rules. Finally, embeddedness in both the ICT environment and the team, with its shared culture, versus embeddedness in different physical environments or non-integration, presents another set of value choices which may favorite some members over others.

In multinational and multicultural teams, project managers need to reconcile the different goals and motivations of employees, which are culturally oriented. They do so by specifying what tradeoffs have been made in a diplomatic way, satisfying some members on a particular issue and others on another issue. For example, a tactful manager may satisfy individualists and challenge seekers by recognizing and incentivizing completion of complex sub-tasks, while generally setting a collective agenda that encourages shared higher-level tasks and facilitates more anonymous question-asking and constructive criticism. Niederman and Tan (2011) reviewed literature on management of global virtual teams, highlighting that points of contention may occur between collectivists and individualists over working together or independently for recognition, as well as between those from low- and high-wage countries who would respond to different incentives. These tensions are part of the work that global software and ICT development teams do, as managers seek to balance differences, and individual team members work together or make decisions about ICT configuration on their own. Besides the embedded individualistic/collectivistic values in technology, a variety of other specific values have been identified as well. For example, multilingualism and accessibility are particular values often embedded in technologies in order to accommodate across social divides and cultural boundaries (Kamwendo, 2008). Similarly, security and control are embedded values that often impede multicultural collaboration by creating barriers (Luo & Olson, 2008).

Implicit cultural values often shape technologies in such a way as to yield unexpected consequences. However, embedded cultural values in technology are sometimes explicitly identified and are therefore intentional. Ardichvili, Maurer, Wei, Wentling, and Stuedemann (2006) identified important cultural considerations in interactions between individuals from Russian, Brazilian, and Chinese cultures that would best facilitate multicultural interaction, such as multimodal ICTs and visibility, so that appropriate expectations of participation patterns by culture would be recognized. In this case, multimodal ICTs included multiple channels for simultaneous text, verbal, and video communication, as well as choice; visibility referred to awareness of a given team member's presence, as well as their context and situational cues, through the multimodal technology. For example, given choices and high detail, individuals from cultures that prioritize face-saving may be uncomfortable with verbal communication in a foreign language and can choose to communicate through text, while those who understand cultural differences can accept a type of participation different from their own habits. These carefully considered cultural choices reflect an attempt to understand the complexities of culture and best facilitate multicultural interaction, because performance is a function of collaboration and usability of technologies across cultural boundaries (Brannen, Garcia, & Thomas, 2009). Development of thoughtful cultural strategies is most effective for multinational organizations, because the ramifications of non-strategic development can be immense (Grachev, 2009) due to lack of coordination and incompatibility.

When cultural values are unintentionally included and are problematic within multicultural spaces, whether because they reflect stereotypes or are not inclusive, modification is possible, as culture shaped the technology in the first place (Bird & Osland, 2005/2006). Cultural tensions within ICT design teams have been well documented (Gibbs, 2009). Trying to understand the cultural composition of technologies, Gibbs (2009) used an organizational tension framework to examine the productive and destructive impacts of team cultural dynamics on their products. He found that transcendence strategies to resolve conflict also have the effect of increasing clarity by developing intuitive and universal solutions, whereas selection and withdrawal strategies constrain choices and embed culturally specific norms within technologies. Furthermore, design teams form a shared cultural identity through collaboration, which can lead to more efficient and effective product development, while groups that do not bond but rather divide work along existing boundaries end up with dysfunctional, incoherent products (Mikawa, Cunnington, & Gaskins, 2009).

Cultures impact technology in both subtle and explicit ways; cultural differences embed values of transparency, accountability, and democracy, as well as the contrasting tendency of top-down control to limit what people can do and see, as a result of cultural hierarchy (Relly & Cuillier, 2010). Additional embedded values, resultant from government choices, include collectivism, "power distance," and "uncertainty avoidance" (Shokef & Erez, 2006). As mentioned in Section 3.1, Arabic culture prefers centralized control. As a result, they maintain strong emphasis on the control of information, which may implicitly impact technology and development in Arab countries, but also produces laws about control of and access to information and technology (Relly & Cuillier, 2010). In fact, Arab countries have fewer access-to-information laws and more centralized control than the average country. Non-Arabic countries with similar political and economic indicators do exhibit similar preferences to control information, which implies that factors other than culture also impact ICT access (Relly & Cuillier, 2010).

3.3   ICT INFRASTRUCTURE IS BUILT, CHANGED, AND ABANDONED BASED ON CULTURAL PRIORITIES

ICT infrastructure is built, changed, and abandoned based on cultural priorities (Bird & Osland, 2005/2006). For the purpose of this discussion, "ICT infrastructure" refers to investment in ICT hardware, software, and networks to support tasks at the group level, and connection at the level of society (Kayan, Fussell, & Setlock, 2006; Luo & Olson, 2008). In situations where multicultural collaboration is desired, ICTs may be modified to include feedback mechanisms, so as to better account for successes, barriers, and cultural attributions (Bird & Osland, 2005/2006). In highly developed contexts, where ICTs are valued for the connectivity they bring to global markets and the educational networks they provide, decision-makers often invest in technical infrastructure that suits their particular experience, whereas this may not be the appropriate technological infrastructure for the needs of the minority or rural cultures that they seek to integrate into more developed networks and supply chains (Gripenberg, Skogseid, Botto, Silli, & Tuuainen, 2004).

When multinational corporations prioritize knowledge and process flows across cultural boundaries, it is logical for them to invest in culturally inclusive systems or changes to ICTs, so that infrastructure supports their goals (Brannen, Garcia, & Thomas, 2009; Gibbs, 2009). Research has revealed that social networking tools, rather than impersonal knowledge bases or communications, facilitate bonding, interaction, and effective, personalized management of distributed multicultural teams (Mikawa, Cunnington, & Gaskins, 2009). Furthermore, embedded collaboration technology within the software suites used by global virtual teams increases self-facilitating, productivity, and interaction (Niederman & Tan, 2011). However, in multicultural contexts, the complexity of competing preferences often leads to complicated, inefficient, exclusionary, or inadequate infrastructure (Gibbs, 2009).

Global development is also culturally determined; as technological accessibility is prioritized for economic development within most cultures and in a multinational global culture, ICTs are invested in based on cultural interests of those in powerful leadership and altruistic positions (James, 2011). In this sense, the values of the privileged class shape technological diffusion based on their charitable interests and global inequality in terms of ICT access grows more complex, with convergence in developing nations and divergence within developed nations (James, 2011). Yet, local development initiatives that better recognize needs and can prioritize for themselves can be successful through investments in cheap, sharable technologies, such as radio information dissemination systems in Malawi (Kamwendo, 2008). At the level of nations, ICT infrastructure is invested in to compete, as well as to collaborate with other cultures (Luo & Olson, 2008).

In order to develop the best ICTs for multicultural interactions, specific consideration must be paid to cultural, social, status, and language uncertainty across boundaries; explicitness, identifiable users, and transparency all help to facilitate multicultural interactions and therefore are important features of infrastructural investments (Setlock, Fussell, Ji, & Culver, 2009). Explicitness of labels and functions is important in ICT interfaces and tools because documentation and specificity decrease variable interpretations. Anonymity of users and low user context also become problematic in multicultural ICT-supported interactions because team members fail to connect as they would in face-to-face interactions; the ability to identify users is important to building trust within teams. Transparency should be valued in ICTs, as it allows distributed users better understanding of the actions and processes of their team. In building a network of ICTs for attribution, negotiation, or decision-making tasks, ICTs should be selected with consideration of characteristics that are best suited to multicultural contexts, in addition to task or process oriented considerations (Setlock, Fussell, Ji, & Culver, 2009).

To sum up, Chapter 3 as a whole approached the relationships between ICT and culture from a socially deterministic perspective, where ICTs are tools that are designed and used by humans. Cultural impact on ICT included impacts on media choice and technical infrastructure, which are influenced by cultural values that are embedded in ICTs. This body of research presented in Chapter 3 conceptualized ICT as products of cultural and multicultural circumstances, emphasizing culturally centric analysis of empirical evidence whereas later, in the next section,

Chapter 4, the reverse assertion will be discussed—ICTs define boundaries of cultural interactions. However, before we focus on the reverse relationships it might be useful to examine the social deterministic approach in comparison with the social informatics approach, as the distinction might not be intuitive to those who hold technological determinism assumptions. The sources of this might be rooted in Kling' (1999) article "What is Social Informatics and Why Does it Matter?" where he starts with the following definition of social informatics:

> *A serviceable working conception of "social informatics" is that it identifies a body of research that examines the social aspects of computerization. A more formal definition is "the interdisciplinary study of the design, uses and consequences of information technologies that takes into account their interaction with institutional and cultural contexts.*

At first it seems like social informatics holds a socially deterministic approach, conceptualizing social informatics as "the study of social aspects of computerization... [focusing on] the use of information technologies in social contexts and the way that social forces and social practices influence information technologies" (Rob Kling Center for Social Informatics, 2013). However, while this is an important part of social informatics research, the social informatics approach does not end there. Instead, social informatics research takes the approach a step further than social determinism, when Kling (1999) suggests that it also incorporate ICTs interaction with context, implying that social informatics includes "the role of information technology in social and organizational change" (Rob Kling Center for Social Informatics, 2013). It is this side of the connection between ICTs and cultures that pushes social informatics to explore these relationships beyond social determinism. ICT here is perceived to have an impact on social change, highlighting also dimensions of technological determinism to be integrated into social informatics. Thus the next section focuses attention on the impact of ICT on culture under the technological determinism approach.

CHAPTER 4

Technological Deterministic Approach to Multiculturalism and ICT: ICT as the Independent Variable

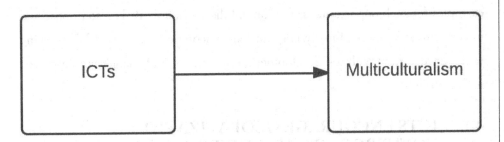

Figure 4.1: Technological deterministic approach to the relationship between ICTs and multiculturalism: ICTs impact multiculturalism.

As has been described, a number of scholars who have sought to understand the relationship between culture and technology found that ICTs serve as the affecter (Figure 4.1) (e.g., Aguilar, 2012; Hampton, Lee, & Her, 2011). Others have sought to tease out how ICTs impact culture, cultural diversity, and multiculturalism (Diamant, Fussell, & Lo, 2008; Purwanto, 2011; Setlock, Quinones, & Fussell, 2007). Some have sought to determine what aspects of culture are affected by ICTs (Cramton & Hinds, 2005; De Laurentis, 2006; Dong & Collaco, 2009; Lauring & Klitmøller, 2010; Saleh, 2011) and others have focused specifically on what aspects of technology actually drives social and cultural dynamics (Hoter, Shonfeld, & Ganayim, 2009; Komito, 2011; Mahdjoubi & Moobela, 2008; Monaka & Mutula, 2010). One significant theoretical construct employed to examine this relationship is the contact hypothesis, which posits that exposure to the 'others' group reduces bias against the group to which individuals are exposed. In this context the online inter-group contact hypothesis model explains how online collaboration increases multiculturalism and cross-cultural cooperation through ICTs that are changing cultural barriers (Hoter, Shonfeld, & Ganayim, 200).

Section 4.1 describes cases in which ICTs encourage globalization, convergence, and divergence, thereby illustrating the roles of ICT in large- and small-scale changes. Section 4.2 presents a general overview of the ways in which ICTs impact socio-cultural dynamics. Section 4.3 presents evidence and arguments for ICT as instigating and creating opportunities for multicultural interactions that would not happen or succeed in their absence; peace and progress are two examples for such opportunities. Section 4.4 discusses how ICTs also impose and remove cultural barriers. Finally, empirical and theoretical analyses of ICT serving as infrastructure for cultural development, interactions, and changes are discussed in Section 4.5.

4.1   ICTS ENCOURAGE GLOBALIZATION, CONVERGENCE, AND DIVERGENCE

From a technological deterministic approach, ICT encourages and facilitates globalization; ICTs also support and enable both cultural convergence and cultural divergence. Globalization is positively associated with development and productivity, when founded in reciprocal exchange and cross-national learning (Cramton & Hinds, 2005). While some convergence increases efficiency, some divergence increases innovation and a balance is important in endeavors such as digital memory institutions, meaning ICT-based archives or repositories for local knowledge and cultural products, and the provision of public services to multicultural publics (De Laurentis, 2006). As ICT enables globalization by reconstructing social boundaries, a hopeful vision of a convergent multicultural global society emerges, yet the obstacles and limitations of barriers between haves and have-nots may simply further diverge cultures toward greater inequality (De Laurentis, 2006; Mahdjoubi & Moobela, 2008; Saleh, 2011).

Convergence and divergence are complex social phenomenon with benefits and costs. Hampton, Lee, and Her (2011) found that co-existent diversity is greater in offline, traditional social interactions than in online interactions. They argue that through ICTs, network expansion leads to divergences into groups that have similar ideas or cultures; these groups subsequently coalescence into more tightly knit, ICT-mediated communities. The trend toward selection of same-culture communities in online worlds helps to maintain ethnocentrism among migrant workers and immigrants, despite the globalized and diverse environments in which they live (Komito, 2011). These dynamic impacts on multiculturalism create conflicting outcomes and unequal distributions of positive global access and negative marginalization (Saleh, 2011).

Convergence is important within organizations seeking to achieve uniform practices, knowledge bases, and culture, yet divergence often occurs based on exogenous cultural boundaries and bounded endogenous multicultural subgroups. Both of these phenomena are enabled by ICTs, indicated by the complexity of their impacts on social structure and work (Lauring & Klitmøller, 2010). Convergence, as a result of ICT, also enables consistent productivity and performance. For example, Setlock, Quinones, and Fussell (2007) found that among pairs of American and Chinese students in different combinations of same-culture and cross-culture dyads, cultural commonalities ceased to affect work because behaviors and expectations converged (Setlock, Quinones, & Fussell, 2007), which enabled consistent levels of performance.

It is significant that a single change in ICT can produce multiple and conflicting social outcomes. There is evidence for both convergence and divergence between indigenous populations participating in a large-scale ICT initiative designed to achieve digital inclusion (Aguilar, 2012). Based on this evidence and trends of growing significance between identity preservation and connection to a larger integrated community, Aguilar (2012) concluded that ICTs facilitate sustainable culture, rather than either cultural preservation or stasis. In this conception, technology fundamentally establishes a new cultural reality by changing understandings of cultures (Aguilar, 2012; Hoter, Shonfeld, & Ganayim, 2009). As people are exposed to new cultures through technology, stereotypes unravel and common ground can be found, which allows individuals to work together to move beyond the tensions that have plagued previous generations from their cultures (Hoter, Shonfeld, & Ganayim, 2009).

4.2   ICTS IMPACT SOCIO-CULTURAL DYNAMICS

Beyond the impact of ICT on globalization, convergence, and divergence, the nature of the impact of ICTs on multiculturalism has been examined both empirically (e.g., Aguilar, 2012) and experimentally (e.g., Diamant, Fussell, & Lo, 2008; Setlock, Quinones, & Fussell, 2007); studies focused on the impact of ICTs in a variety of contexts, including global virtual teams (Cramton & Hinds, 2005) and sociopolitical initiatives, such as digital inclusion projects (Aguilar, 2012; Saleh, 2011). This research concludes that ICTs both directly and indirectly impact socio-cultural dynamics (Hampton, Lee, & Her, 2011; Setlock, Quinones, & Fussell, 2007); these impacts are empirical manifestations of the technological deterministic assumptions.

For example, Aguilar (2012) examined ICT as an independent variable in relationship to cultural diversity, and found that 1) technology, cultural identity, and diversity are not all directly related, but since technology can impact cultural identity, it also can impact diversity as a result; 2) information resources and ICTs can be configured to support cultural identity and diversity; and 3) cultural identity and diversity can be impacted or changed through ICT configuration. In this intensive qualitative study of two indigenous populations in Brazil participating in the Indios online initiative, the relationship between cultural identity and technology followed different trajectories. While one group utilized information technology access to participate in globalization and integrate with other cultures, the second group used technology to clearly define their own cultural identity and maintain their independence (Aguilar, 2012). Whereas the project was designed to increase diversity of participation in the information society through technology, only one group directly did this, but the experience of the second group illustrates a more complex relationship between diversity, technology, and cultural identity. Therefore, it becomes clear that ICTs impact groups and their boundaries in two opposing directions; they homogenize and fragment multicultural groups as well as help spanning boundaries and creating them (Lauring & Klitmøller, 2010). The relationship between ICTs and fragmented multicultural societies is complex. On one hand, society benefits through development and advancing multicultural contacts, individual cultures, and multicultural goals; on the other hand, ICTs have the potential to harm multicultural society through increased convergence of distinct cultural groups or social un-structuring (Purwanto, 2011). In this sense, ICT creates opportunities both for same culture and multicultural interactions.

Additionally, ICTs increase group performance and social intelligence, which in turn decreases ethnocentrisms. ICTs also increase intercultural participation and improve collaboration (Diamant, Fussell, & Lo, 2008; Dong & Collaco, 2009; Setlock, Quinones, & Fussell, 2007). More specifically, ICT enables exposure and unique social learning opportunities to increase social intelligence. These opportunities are particularly enabled by synchronous and rich-media technologies, as these ICTs reveal more nuanced information about the feelings, thoughts, and behaviors of those with whom one interacts (Dong & Collaco, 2009; Setlock, Quinones, & Fussell, 2007). Research has indicated that ethnocentrism decreases as social intelligence increases (Dong & Collaco, 2009); this then increases intercultural participation and multicultural collaboration. In some cases ICTs have more impact than do cultural biases on performance, though both are correlated with performance; ICT facilitates shared-culture partnerships and multicultural partnerships to complete given tasks in teams (Diamant, Fussell, & Lo, 2008).

Furthermore, there is evidence that different ICTs—such as video versus audio versus instant messaging—affect cultural biases differently (Setlock, Quinones, & Fussell, 2007), in addition to the impact of ICTs on multicultural collaboration and group performance. Consequently the choice of ICT medium indirectly impacts also performance as well (Shachaf, 2008). For example, Diamant, Fussell, and Lo (2008) found that group cohesion and multicultural interactions were shallowest and least productive without auditory or visual cues when groups were coordinating and collaborating by instant messaging alone. This multicultural engagement is consistent with work on social intelligence and intercultural interaction because using audio-visual media for interaction provide more behavioral and emotional understanding to build mutual understanding (Dong & Collaco, 2009).

ICTs also impact socio-cultural dynamics not only at the group level but also at the macro-level by supporting diversification, glocalization,[3] and globalization (Hampton, Lee, & Her, 2011). At this national and multinational scale, ICTs serve important cultural roles in broadcasting ideas to make advocacy uniquely effective at a massive scale. Social media, in particular, supports diverse networks and interactions by creating opportunities for traditional social activities in mediated environments to extend their reach at a larger scale than was previously possible. As social connections are sustained by minimizing the disruptions of geography, technology is dramatically affecting multiculturalism by changing the nature and frequency of major social trends, such as migration (Komito, 2011). ICTs also help to fix past social ills in multicultural societies. For example, by establishing equality in multilingual resources in Botswana through ICT, it enables the removal of cost and efficiency barriers to multilingual governance (Monaka & Mutula, 2010).

However, ICTs also bring opposite impacts on society. There is evidence that over time ICTs transform traditional cultures, leaving some unrecognizable and highly integrated with majority cultures and others more identifiable (Purwanto, 2011). For example, in the case of Indonesia, the introduction of ICT-mediated interactions exacerbated social tensions regarding religious standards of behavior and social norms; the Internet allowed for liberalization of the behaviors of young people to the chagrin of religious leaders, while at the same time providing a space for cultural identity formation through ethnocentric online communities (Purwanto, 2011).

Despite those socio-cultural conflicts, many developing countries, such as Egypt, Ghana, and South Africa, recognize the transformative potential of ICT in terms of education and socio-economic development to be undeniably desirable (Saleh, 2011). According to Saleh (2011), Egypt, for example, has invested

---

[3]   Glocalization is a combination of the words "globalization" and "localization." It is used to describe the accommodation of a product that was distributed globally for the local market adaptation. The glocalized product may conform to local culture, laws, customs, or consumer preferences.

extensively in ICT and access initiatives. Internet access is free within the country, though low literacy and computer ownership limit use of this service. ICTs have structured collaboration and coordination between the public and private sectors, which has led to economic growth. A South African initiative provides a more successful example, with increasing use of ICT and increasing e-democratic participation, though with unequal gains along demographic lines (Saleh, 2011). Yet, Ghana, also seeking improvements, has seen the lowest levels of benefit and use, likely because their national infrastructure is the least developed; still, their initiative seeks to improve the country and raise earning potential by cheaply distributing information and online educational tools to their population (Saleh, 2011).

4.3   ICTS ESTABLISH OPPORTUNITIES FOR MULTICULTURAL INTERACTION, PEACE, AND PROGRESS

A fundamental manifestation of the impact of ICTs is the establishment of opportunities for multicultural interactions, peace, and progress. From a technological deterministic approach, ICTs enable global, multi-national organizations to conduct business effectively through international collaboration. Multicultural interactions within organizations are shaped and structured by the specific affordances of given technologies, which impose standards and parameters for these interactions (Lauring & Klitmøller, 2010). ICT creates knowledge bases and sharing mechanisms to facilitate decision-making within multicultural groups in ways that can benefit diverse members, sustain their interactions, and improve their performance (Mahdjoubi & Moobela, 2008; Shachaf, 2008). As ICT increases and expands social opportunity, the number of connections an individual has can increase, and with more expansive and dense networks, cultural diversity increases (Hampton, Lee, & Her, 2011). Because diversity and multiculturalism at the global level are limited without technology, manipulation of technology to better facilitate diversity becomes important to support global business, connect migrants to their friends and families, and encourage international cooperation. Even within highly diverse local communities, the social distance between cultures can still be great, and, in these cases, ICTs can be used to overcome distance and bring multicultural publics together (Mahdjoubi & Moobela, 2008).

It is critical to emphasize why multicultural interactions are important in a globalized era because, while ethnocentrism is common and perhaps even natural, teams are more productive and effective when cultural mediation through technology increases interaction between and salience of diverse subgroups (Cramton & Hinds, 2005). Avoidance of cultural fragmentation and exacerbation of tensions, which are distinctly possible (i.e., Purwanto, 2011), matters to the achievement of peace, progress, and social justice among cultures. Aguilar's aforementioned study of indigenous digital inclusion serves as an example: the historically insular and geographically isolated Pankararus people of Brazil were shown to be increasingly employing technology through the Indios online program to develop economically and educationally, as well as to integrate themselves with other cultures through digital bridges (Aguilar, 2012). Cultural minorities can be integrated into larger social structures through ICT, partaking in the economy and participatory politics, despite difference and low physical proximity, all while maintaining their cultural identities. These mechanisms are promising for the future of respectful cultural co-existence.

ICT establishes opportunities that can support peace. In addition to the possibilities for isolated cultures to interact beyond geographic limits that were in the past insurmountable, there are also possibilities for cultures historically at odds with one another to interact in a productive and hopeful way (Hoter, Shonfeld, & Ganayim, 2009). Toward this end, Hoter, Shonfeld, and Ganayim (2009) studied an online learning project based in Israel that paired Arabic and Jewish students in a structured, ICT-mediated interactive space under the premises of the contact hypothesis in order to reduce cultural tension and provide students the opportunity to benefit from multicultural perspectives. At the end of the study, students reported high satisfaction and increased levels of trust and communication over the course of the project; the researchers identified the collaborative nature of the environment as reducing bias through exposure and stymying competition between cultures by ensuring equal status among participants (Hoter, Shonfeld, &

Ganayim, 2009). While the outcome of this study may be somewhat exceptional, it illustrates that exposure to other cultures increases understanding and intercultural collaboration can be more successful over time, as a result of sharing cultural knowledge and preferences.

These opportunities are uniquely possible through ICTs, and the properties of the ICTs themselves create cultural changes by reducing animosity and misunderstanding. Interaction across cultural boundaries is not only important to peace and progress in the future, but also to righting past wrongs and creating an equal footing for all cultures. Through multicultural interactions established by ICTs, marginalized cultures can reap the benefits of idea and knowledge exchange to meet their needs (Monaka & Mutula, 2010). Social justice may not be achieved purely through communication, but information sharing contributes to increasing equality in health, education, and finance. For example, as ICTs create opportunities for multicultural interaction, economic development has increased in Egypt, educational opportunities have increased across the African continent, and small businesses have been able to reach global markets (Saleh, 2011). On the other hand, many ICT-based development initiatives in Africa have struggled and show little in the way of gains (Saleh, 2011).

While avoidance of cultural tensions is important, as mentioned, to achieve peace and progress, ICTs do not exclusively produce positive social change. Contrary to the support of multicultural cooperation and positive interaction, the opportunities for multicultural interaction created by ICTs actually exacerbate many social problems between diametrically opposed cultures by creating spaces for conflict (Purwanto, 2011). At times, interactions have proved frustrating as skill, communication, and literacy gaps have made multicultural interaction socially uncomfortable for the disadvantaged (Saleh, 2011). Specifically, in educational settings in Ghana and Egypt, illiteracy and unfamiliarity with technology have served as powerful barriers to participation in new educational initiatives, which have provided access without teaching the fundamental skills necesssary to take advantage of these opportunities (Saleh, 2011). Thus, ICT's impact on interaction can also be adverse if the tools implemented are tailored only to other cultural situations (Mahdjoubi & Moobela, 2008).

4.4   ICTS REMOVE OR IMPOSE CULTURAL BARRIERS

The technologically deterministic approach asserts that multiculturalism and cultural differentiation both result from and are shaped by ICT influences. Different technological configurations, features, constraints, and infrastructure create or remove cultural barriers. Section 4.4.1 emphasizes the boundaries created within and between cultures, as a result of ICTs, whereas Section 4.4.2 illustrates how and when ICTs diminish cultural barriers, opening paths for positive multicultural interaction as well as reduced cultural identity.

4.4.1   BARRIER ESTABLISHMENT AND CREATION

Through ICTs, cultural barriers are established between the connected and the periphery, as well as between those who participate in the collective cultural production and those who seek to remain or become distinct (De Laurentis, 2006). Cultural barriers also develop into self-contained networks with a common culture around like-minded individuals because ICT makes it is easier to draw like-minded individuals, as there is a larger population, and bring them together around very specific common interests (Hampton, Lee, & Her, 2011). ICTs also allow for the construction of new multicultural barriers along collaborative subgroup lines, which is critical to information exchange, inclusive contact among members, social support, equal status, engagement, perception of interdependence, and cross-national learning.

Furthermore, cultural barriers emerge as technology practices from one location within an organization are applied as is universally. This practice has the effect of enabling exclusion based on language or by increasing the social distance between other cultures, such as along Eastern and Western cultural divides, and at the same time drawing similar cultures closer together (Lauring & Klitmøller, 2010). Therefore, the imposition of cultural barriers, such as language-specific social networks, preserves cultural identity within a global economy.

The significance of keeping these barriers in a multicultural world is to pre-serve small communities within a global networked community (Komito, 2011). Some barriers are still important to successful group work in that they reduce tensions produced by overt differences without structured commonality (Cramton & Hinds, 2005). While social fragmentation may have positive impacts within groups (Cramton & Hinds, 2005), on a larger scale, however, social fragmentation inhibits knowledge flow in businesses by decreasing communication effectiveness and reducing cross-boundary interaction (Lauring & Klitmøller, 2010).

4.4.2 BARRIER REDUCTION AND ELIMINATION

While ICTs have the potential to impose and create new barriers, ICTs can also remove barriers. ICT diminishes local boundaries, creating a global space for a digital, knowledge-based economy (De Laurentis, 2006). Specifically ICTs re-move barriers by diminishing the adverse effects of migration and enhancing the process by extending social ties to ease the complications of migration. ICTs also help facilitate advanced planning for migration, and support bridging dispersed individuals with their native cultures, allowing for continued participation de-spite distance (Komito, 2011). This makes the distance between local and global less culturally significant, which has positive social implications. Moreover, ICT positively impacts multiculturalism by eliminating ethnocentric and conflicting barriers (Monaka & Mutula, 2010).

The removal of cultural barriers is important to establishing multicultural understanding between participants (Dong & Collaco, 2009; Mahdjoubi & Moo-bela, 2008). Yet greater understanding of the boundary-spanning potential of ICTs to better facilitate intercultural collaboration is much needed (Dong & Collaco, 2009). Specifically, as ICT intervention deconstructs cultural barriers in a signif-icant way, by minimizing bias, removing stigmas, and reducing prejudice through increasing exposure between conflicting cultural groups (Hoter, Shonfeld, & Ganayim, 2009). Multimedia spaces, in particular for multicultural decision-mak-ing, provide opportunities to interact and articulate group interests without the cultural and geographical barriers that separate groups from interacting face-to-face (Mahdjoubi & Moobela, 2008). Furthermore, ICTs can structure contact as boundary crossing agents to overcome the adverse effects of boundaries created by other technologies (Lauring & Klitmøller, 2010; Monaka & Mutula, 2010), creating a complex and reciprocal relationship between ICTs and boundaries. ICTs allow international, distributed collaboration by removing geographic barriers, social cues, and cultural barriers.

Moreover, ICTs also negatively impact multiculturalism by shoring up conflicting boundaries or creating new ones (Purwanto, 2011). Harmful cultural boundaries created by ICT include inconveniences to certain groups due to mis-identification or access restrictions, costs of participation, means of participation, and community distance (Mahdjoubi & Moobela, 2008). For example, ICTs in Indonesia have served to inflame previously unspoken and indirect conflicts between generations and traditional cultures versus a rapidly modernizing culture (Purwanto, 2011). ICTs have removed barriers preventing large scale cultural conflict and reinforced differences between cultures by accelerating modernization and exposing rural, traditional cultures to contemporary, urban cultural phenomenon, such as non-traditional gender roles and sexual promiscuity (Purwanto, 2011). This is harmful in that these conflicts prevent the benefits from multicultural interactions from being realized (Purwanto, 2011).

4.5 ICTS AS INFRASTRUCTURE FOR CULTURAL DEVELOPMENT AND CHANGE

ICT provides technological infrastructure for cultural stability, maintenance, development and change; it provides infrastructure for creation and maintenance of online communities, cultural identity, and development as it enables bridging over geographical boundaries (for migrant groups) and language barriers. Certain ICTs are designed, from the beginning, to have social impact and to increase multicultural connections. They do so by structuring interactions and bridging connections at both wider and more specific ranges. Yet, at the same time, there is evidence that specificity of ICT-supported interaction decreases overall diversity by allowing people to find more people like themselves (Hampton, Lee, & Her, 2011). This variability in network inclusion allows for specific cultural boundaries to develop or be bridged. ICTs structure socio-cultural interactions and changes (Purwanto, 2011) by, for example, digitizing and monetizing culture, thereby altering it through the synthesis of cultural identities and exploitation of creative productions (De Laurentis, 2006). There is also evidence that some cultural exploitation and disenfranchisement is unintentional in ICT design. For example, technologies specifically designed to facilitate shared decision-making in fractured multicultural communities often continue to exclude minority members due to barriers that go unnoticed by members of advantaged communities, such as participation costs in terms of literacy and technological experience (Mahdjoubi & Moobela, 2008).

ICTs provide the network infrastructure to form overarching cultural paradigms; these are enabled through ICTs and formed by ICTs. The best examples to illustrate these cultures include meta-indigenous culture (Aguilar, 2012) or online communities such as multicultural learning communities (Hoter, Shonfeld, & Ganayim, 2009). These technologies can support existing networked connections for collaboration and diversity and create new ones (Cramton & Hinds, 2005; Hampton, Lee, & Her, 2011). In total, ICTs create a new digital economy in which the opportunities for cultural production greatly expand, yet which also exacerbates cultural disparities between those connected and those not. In this sense ICTs also structure, develop, and stabilize culture and society (De Laurentis, 2006). Because of their networked and interactive nature, ICTs provide infrastructure for cultural development and change by supporting interactions, facilitating connections, and creating opportunities between members of different cultural orientations. Specific affordances, such as asynchronicity across time zones, support for multilingual environments, and multimodal channels further contribute to the infrastructural role of ICTs.

ICTs provide also infrastructure for cultural identity construction and maintenance (Komito, 2011). For example, auditory and visual ICTs are the most common ICTs used by Polish and Indonesian migrants in Ireland, who seek to sustain strong social ties despite the geographic breadth of their social network.

ICT supports cultural infrastructure in that it makes multicultural connections that would not otherwise be feasible (Setlock, Quinones, & Fussell, 2007).

ICTs also uniquely enable multicultural interactions across language boundaries; technologies enable linguistic technologies to be compatible, uniting marginalized groups with majority cultures within nations and bridging marginalized groups with the outside world (Monaka & Mutula, 2010). It is not possible to scale such interactions without technology because international, national, and regional institutions cannot support local culture and knowledge exchange through human or cultural means alone (Monaka & Mutula, 2010). ICTs provide support for cultural infrastructure, connecting the developed and developing nations in a global network for communication, collaboration, and cooperation (Saleh, 2011).

To sum up, Chapter 4 reveals the evidence base for a technologically deterministic conception of interaction between ICT and multiculturalism. From this perspective, technology drives multiculturalism and shapes cultural interactions, with both constructive and conflicting outcomes. As Section 4.1 demonstrates, ICTs yield new cultural distributions and arrangements, ranging from reduction of cultural differentiation to increased separation. As socio-cultural dynamics are changed by technological constraints and transformations (Section 4.2), opportunities for intercultural interaction, peace, and progress are shaped (Section 4.3), largely because ICTs are infrastructure for cultural interactions (Section 4.5) and cultural barriers or boundaries are redistributed (Section 4.4). This body of research importantly summarizes the mechanisms through which ICTs have impact and are not simply tools or channels. This is important to consider with respect to ICT implementation. In some ways, though technological determinism is a unique ideology, it complements a social informatics view by considering the technology in isolation from what may impact it. This is useful to empirically test causality and to complement ICT development and adoption strategies by those who narrowly conceive of ICT as tools; social informatics synthesizes social and technical shaping conceptions, and, when not applied predictively, technological determinism can be employed as a component of a more balanced and inclusive conceptualization of bidirectional impacts.

However, technological determinism is limited in that it: 1) reduces ICT to its hardware, software, and structure components; 2) denies the considerable and confounding impact of context on human interactions with technology; 3) ignores its own internally inconsistent and often incorrect expectations for simple, direct effects; and 4) fails to acknowledge the influences of the individuals, teams, and cultures which produce technologies (Kling, 1999). However technological determinism generated much criticism that served as the driving force behind sociotechnical models, and social informatics as well. These aimed to address the relationships between ICT and people, groups, organizations, and society, while explaining their paradoxical, cyclical, co-evolving, and mutually shaped nature.

CHAPTER 5

Conclusions

The relationships between ICT and multiculturalism attract much scholarly attention and while scholars agree that this relationship is of significant importance and needs to be further explored, they hold different assumptions regarding the nature of the relationship based on three unique approaches. While strong evidence exists for each of the three conceptualizations of the relationship between culture and ICTs as independent and alternative paradigms, the argument can also be made that the social informatics perspective synthesizes the evidence used to support the other models. In this sense, the two deterministic models can be integrated into an aggregated, bidirectional global model (e.g., Diamant, Fussell, & Lo, 2009; Setlock, Fussell, & Neuwirth, 2004; Setlock, Fussell, Ji, & Culver, 2009; Wang, Fussell, & Setlock, 2009). Furthermore, the dynamic nature of a mutually shaping interaction can explain contradictory prevailing trends in specific contexts, as used to support these one-directional models (e.g., Dawes, Gharawi, & Burke, 2012; Lievrouw, 1998; Nurmi, Bosch-Sijtsema, Sivunen, & Fruchter, 2009). In joining these arguments with the respective bodies of research, the social informatics perspective is supported even further.

While the two deterministic models are in opposition, the evidence supporting either one cannot be discarded as irrelevant for understanding the relationships between ICTs and culture. Yet it is possible to accept both of these influences together as true, which supports a mutually shaping model, manifested as a social informatics perspective. The evidence that both deterministic approaches bring to light complements the other within a third, more holistic approach—social informatics. Each of the two is a necessary, yet modified component of the combined bi-directional approach.

Social determinism as an approach is useful as it focuses on the ways that humans shape and use technological products; this perspective is useful in illustrating how technologies are used as tools within cultures. Within this paradigm,

ICTs are conceptualized as social and cultural products, emphasizing the cultural context of design and use. Yet it fails to acknowledge that technologies also impact social configurations and cultural interactions in ways that are not a direct result from the initial cultural choices.

Therefore, the technological determinism approach is also useful, as it focuses on the ways technologies and their attributes—including configurations, affordances, and modes—impact society and cultural interactions. Following this understanding, technology drives social and cultural change and stasis, producing both positive and negative outcomes; this is important because ICTs are more than simply tools. They are systems that extend beyond combinations of hardware and software to include systems support and other users; the dynamic and complex nature of sociotechnical systems, as a description of ICT, produces a sense of agency through uncontrolled and unanticipated outcomes (Kling, 1999). Yet this ideological construction of the relationship between ICTs and multiculturalism fails to account for the values and assumptions underlying technological design, implementation and use choices. This approach can only provide partial explanation for ICT design, implementation, and use, since technologies do not simply spring into being, born of previous technologies; they do so in a socio-cultural context.

Social informatics balances the evidence on either side by acknowledging complexity, dynamics, and feedback loops between various forces. This perspective is both integrative and flexible, accepting multiple models—bidirectional, cyclical, and mediated modes—of interaction. Data supporting both other models are comprehensible and complementary from this viewpoint, as they may simply represent instances in which one variable exerts a greater or more immediately noticeable impact.

Scholarly works on ICT and multiculturalism illustrate that cultures and ICTs do not simply interact linearly; culture shapes the technology through values embedded in the design and the meaning and use of technology are culture dependent. Technology in turn impacts the culture from which it originated and impacts another culture during the implementation process. Furthermore, ICT and multiculturalism shape each other concurrently, with multiple cultural perspectives co-producing technologies or ICT configurations and new technologies exerting socio-cultural impacts. Understanding that these bi-directional relationships are more complex is extremely beneficial to guide multicultural collaboration in work, research, governance, and social contexts. The social informatics approach appropriately balances the contextual nature of each interaction and the complex, dynamic, and unexpected outcomes of ICT supported multicultural collaboration, at both the group and society levels.

Empirical evidence for socially and technologically deterministic models provides an incomplete representation of the relationships between culture and ICTs. These deterministic models perhaps represent either methodological limitations to longitudinal data gathering, which could possibly reveal mutual interactions over time, or contexts in which either the social or technical force was less evident, though not absent. While social and cultural determinism can be beneficial at the early stages of ICT design, which is frequently driven by technological determinism, technological determinism may explain challenges in the implementation and use stages that are often more focused on stakeholders. The social informatics approach can help integrate the two and improve ICT design, implementation, and use.

5.1   IMPLICATIONS

These three conceptualizations explain specific outcomes and expectations based on their own sets of assumptions, but in aggregate can empirically ground many decisions regarding ICTs across cultures. As discussed in the introduction, issues of multiculturalism and ICT extend far beyond the teams and development initiatives covered here, to include such diverse contexts as scholarly collaboration and international economic negotiation. However, this synthesis holds relevant implications for decision-making on collaborative business ventures, regarding both teams and organizational structure; ICT access initiatives for community, national, and regional development; and the designs of future technologies to reflect sociocultural preferences (Schadewitz & Zakaria, 2009; Shachaf, 2008).

Applications of this research inform business decisions in global, multicultural, and collaborative organizations. Based on increased understanding of alternative mechanisms for the relationships between ICT and multiculturalism, organizations can make more informed decisions about global collaboration, team structure, and technological investment to improve their effectiveness and impact in a global society. Global businesses must consider that diversity spans issues of power relations, rationalities, infrastructural preferences, and status-seeking, complicating structure as much as interaction in terms of compatibility issues (Barrett, Jarvenpaa, Silva, & Walsham, 2003). Within team contexts, leaders need to consider differences in agenda setting and prioritization, communication style and media preferences, as well as coordinating tasks; teams are most successful when an internal group culture can mask underlying differences in national or ethnic culture (Hsin Hsin, Shuang-Shii, & Shu Han, 2011; Naor, Liderman, & Schroeder, 2010), by establishing common culture and consistent use of technology (Setlock, Fussell, Ji, & Culer, 2009).

ICT access initiatives can also be more intelligently and carefully designed and evaluated based on this knowledge. Community and national development initiatives pertaining to ICTs can benefit from an understanding that technologies may have cultural consequences or benefits (Cozzens, 2012), with particularly complex impacts on indigenous cultures (Aguilar, 2012). The implication for designs of these initiatives is that investing without carefully identifying goals and factors needed for success will have cultural repercussions in addition to failing (Saleh, 2011). Initiatives must be suited to the context (Kamwendo, 2008), rather than laterally transferred from other successful initiatives, and be grounded in sound policy (Gebremichael & Jackson, 2006). Yet the introduction of ICTs cannot overcome all inequalities and previous injustices without adequate attention to the context (Papaioannou, 2011).

Furthermore, the design and development of ICTs can be improved by considering the evidence provided by these various studies for the alternate models of impact and influence between technology and culture. This improvement results from an understanding that technology will impact stakeholders on a socio-cultural level and be impacted by the cultural dynamics of the creators. Specifically, this has implications for knowledge management systems, for example: knowledge management systems should reflect the results of cultural needs assessments, rather than preconceived notions about how to best deliver information (Ardichvilli, Maurer, Li, Wentling, & Studemann, 2006), and ICTs intended for multicultural collaboration should include multiple media in concert (Shachaf, 2008).

What this synthesis does in aggregating scholarship in support of these three models is to clarify the differences in strands of conversation surrounding technology and multiculturalism and illustrate how these differences are useful and can be bridged. These ideologies—social informatics, social determinism, and technological determinism—often differentiate researchers addressing similar questions, yet the boundaries between them can be spanned by considering areas of overlap and their combined implications for practical decision-making. While there have historically been three mostly separate conversations, with an exception being overt conflict between these paradigms, ICT-supported multicultural interactions and initiatives would benefit from increased conversation between scholars in all areas. This synthesis makes explicit the areas in which each paradigm has advantages, paradigms are complementary, and there is common ground.

5.2   FUTURE RESEARCH

This body of research leaves a number of lingering questions and gaps in understanding multicultural issues in ICTs, which are critical to planning and development, in an increasingly globalized world, on cultural, economic, and political levels. For example, it is important to elucidate the role of ICTs in the globalization process, power and politics, cultural diversity and local social arrangements, and social networks and institutions, as well as the role of culture in technology diffusion and deployment (Barrett, Jarvenpaa, Silva, & Walsham, 2003). It is also important that future research better conceptualizes and enumerates mediating variables associated with socio-cultural ICT interaction (Mutula, 2005).

Specific unanswered questions include: What is the effect of distinction between out-group and in-group cultures within communities (Ardichvili, Maurer,

Wei, Wentling, & Stuedemann, 2006)? Do cultural distinction and ICTs produce glocalization, rather than globalization (Kaye & Little, 2000)? How do the causes of socio-cultural inequalities compare to the causes of digital inequality (Oyedemi, 2009)? Can solutions to digital inequality contribute to increased social equality (Papaioannou, 2011)? How can social and digital infrastructure be integrated (Sassi, 2005)? How do social boundaries compare to cultural boundaries in ICT-supported intercultural interaction (Dong & Collaco, 2009)? What, aside from culture, produces fault lines within global virtual teams (Hung & Nguyen, 2008)? What specific cultural components produce different ICT preferences and how do cultural differences produce different technological interests (Niederman & Tan, 2011)?

References

Adler, N. J. (1983a). A typology of management studies involving culture. *Journal of International Business Studies*, 14(2), 29-47. DOI: 10.1057/palgrave.jibs.8490517.

Aguilar, A. (2012). Cultural/diversity identity in cyberspace: Informational practices and digital inclusion in Brazil. *Informacao & Sociedade-Estudos*, 22(1), 121-128.

Akman, I., Yazici, A., Mishra, A., & Arifoglu, A. (2005). E-Government: A global view and an empirical evaluation of some attributes of citizens, *Government Information Quarterly*, 22(2), 239-257, ISSN 0740-624X, DOI: 10.1016/j.giq.2004.12.001.

Ardichvili, A., Maurer, M., Wei, L., Wentling, T., & Stuedemann, R. (2006). Cultural influences on knowledge sharing through online communities of practice. *Journal of Knowledge Management*, 10, 94-107. DOI: 10.1108/13673270610650139.

Barrett, M., Jarvenpaa, S., Silva, L., & Walsham, G. (2003). ICTs, Globalization and local diversity. *Communications of AIS*, 11, 486-497.

Bimber, B. (1990). Karl Marx and the Three Faces of Technological Determinism. *Social Studies Of Science*, 20(2), 333-351. DOI: 10.1177/030631290020002006.

Bird, A., & Osland, J. S. (2005/2006). Making sense of intercultural collaboration. *International Studies of Management & Organization*, 35(4), 115-132.

Boast, R., Bravo, M., & Srinivasan, R. (2007). Return to Babel: Emergent diversity, digital resources, and local knowledge. *The Information Society: An International Journal*, 23(5), 395-403. DOI: 10.1080/01972240701575635.

Brannen, M. Y., Garcia, D., & Thomas, D. (2009). Biculturals as natural bridges for intercultural communication and collaboration. In Fussell, S. et al (Eds.),

Proceedings of the 2009 International Workshop on Intercultural Collaboration (pp. 207-210). New York, NY: ACM. DOI: 10.1145/1499224.1499257.

Cohen, S. G., & Bailey, D. E. (1997). What makes teams work: Group effectiveness research from the shop floor to the executive suite. *Journal of Management*, 23(3), 239-291. DOI: 10.1177/014920639702300303.

Cozzens, S. E. (2012). Social cohesion at the global level: The roles of science and technology. *Science & Public Policy* (SPP), 39(5), 557-561. DOI: 10.1093/scipol/scs067.

Cramton, C. D. & Hinds, P. J. (2005). Subgroup dynamics in internationally distributed teams: Ethnocentrism or cross-national learning? *Research in Organizational Behavior*, 26, 231-263. DOI: 10.1016/S0191-3085(04)26006-3.

Dafoulas, G., & Macaulay, L. (2001). Investigating cultural differences in virtual software teams. *The Electronic Journal on Information Systems in Developing Countries*, 7(4), 1-14.

Daily, B. F., & Steiner, R. L. (1998). The influence of group decision support systems on contribution and commitment levels in multicultural and culturally homogeneous decision-making groups. *Computers in Human Behavior*, 14(1), 147-162. DOI: 10.1016/S0747-5632(97)00037-X.

Daily, B., Whatley, A., Ash, S. R., & Steiner, R. L. (1996). The effects of a group decision support system on culturally diverse and culturally homogeneous group decision making. *Information & Management*, 30, 281-289. DOI: 10.1016/S0378-7206(96)01062-2.

Dawes, S. S., Gharawi, M. A., & Burke, G. B. (2012). Transnational public sector knowledge networks: Knowledge and information sharing in a multi-dimensional context, *Government Information Quarterly*, 29(1), S112-S120, ISSN 0740-624X, DOI: 10.1016/j.giq.2011.08.002.

De Laurentis, C. (2006). Digital knowledge exploitation: ICT, memory institutions and innovation from cultural assets. *Journal of Technology Transfer*, 31(1), 77. DOI:10.1007/s10961-005-5014-6.

d'Haenens, L. (2003). ICT in multicultural society. *Gazette: International Journal for Communication Studies*, 65(4/5), 401. DOI: 10.1177/0016549203654006.

Diamant, E. I., Fussell, S. R., & Lo, F.-L. (2008). "Where did we turn wrong?" Unpacking the effects of cultura and technology on attributions of team performance. *Proceedings of CSCW 2008*. New York, NY: ACM. DOI: 10.1145/1460563.1460625.

Diamant, E. I., Fussell, S. R., & Lo, F. L. (2009). Collaborating across cultural and technological boundaries: Team culture and information use in a map navigation task. In Fussell, S. et al (Ed.), *Proceedings of the 2009 International Workshop on Intercultural Collaboration* (pp. 175-184). New York, NY: ACM. DOI: 10.1145/1499224.1499251.

Dong, Q., & Collaco, C. M. (2009). Overcome ethnocentrism and increase intercultural collaboration by developing social intelligence. In Fussell, S. et al (Eds.), *Proceedings of the 2009 International Workshop on Intercultural Collaboration* (pp. 215-218). New York, NY: ACM. DOI: 10.1145/1499224.1499259.

Duarte, D. L., & Snyder, N. T. (1999). *Mastering virtual teams: Strategies, tools, and techniques that succeed*. San-Francisco, CA: Jossey-Bass Publishers.

Earley, P. C., & Mosakowski, E. (2000). Creating hybrid teams cultures: An empirical test of transnational teams functioning. *Academy of Management Journal*, 43(1), 26-49. DOI: 10.2307/1556384.

Easterby-Smith, M. & Malina, D. (1999). Cross-cultural collaborative research: Toward reflexivity. *Academy of Management Journal*, 42, 76-86. DOI: 10.2307/256875.

Falkheimer, J., & Heide, M. (2009). Crisis communication in a new world: Reaching multicultural publics through old and new media. *NORDICOM Review*, 30(1), 55-66.

Fleischmann, K. R. (forthcoming). Social informatics, human values, and ICT design. In P. Fichman & H. Rosenbaum (Eds). *Social Informatics: Past, Present and Future*. Cambridge Scholars Publishing.

Fleischmann, K. R. (2007). Digital Libraries with Embedded Values: Combining Insights from LIS and Science and Technology Studies. *Library Quarterly*, 77(4), 409-427. DOI: 10.1086/520997.

Fleischmann, K.R., Wallace, W. A., & Grimes, J. M. (2011). How Values Can Reduce Conflicts in the Design Process: Results from a Multi-Site Mixed-Method Field Study. *Proceedings of the 74th Annual Meeting of the American Society for Information Science and Technology*, New Orleans, LA. DOI: 10.1002/meet.2011.14504801147.

Gebremichael, M. D., & Jackson, J. W. (2006). Bridging the gap in Sub-Saharan Africa: A holistic look at information poverty and the region's digital divide, *Government Information Quarterly*, 23(2), 267-280, ISSN 0740-624X, DOI: 10.1016/j.giq.2006.02.011.

Gibbs, J. L. (2009). Dialectics in a global software team: Negotiating tensions across time, space, and culture. *Human Relations*, 62(6), 905-935. DOI: 10.1177/0018726709104547.

Gibson, C. B., & Gibbs, J. L. (2006). Unpacking the concept of virtuality: The effects of geographic dispersion, electronic dependence, dynamic structure, and national diversity on team innovation. *Administrative Science Quarterly*, 51, 451-495. DOI: 10.2189/asqu.51.3.451.

Gigerenzer, G., & Gaissmaier, W. (2011). Heuristic decision making. *Annual Review Of Psychology*, 62, 451-482. DOI: 10.1146/annurev-psych-120709-145346.

Grachev, M. (2009). Culture-sensitive global strategies. In Fussell, S. et al (Ed.), *Proceedings of the 2009 International Workshop on Intercultural Collaboration* (pp. 229-232). New York, NY: ACM. DOI: 10.1145/1499224.1499263.

Grint, K., & S. Woolgar. (1997). *The machine at work: Technology, work, and organization.* Cambridge, UK: Polity.

Gripenberg, P., Skogseid, I., Botto, F., Silli, A., & Tuunainen, V. K. (2004). Entering the European information society: Four rural development projects, *The Information Society: An International Journal,* 20:1, 3-14. Preview. DOI: 10.1080/01972240490269807.

Gudykunst, W. B., Matsumoto, Y., Ting-Toomey, S., Nishida, T., Kim, K., & Heyman, S. (1996). The influence of cultural individualism-collectivism, self-construals, and individual values on communication styles across cultures. *Human Communication Research,* 22, 510-543. DOI: 10.1111/j.1468-2958.1996.tb00377.x.

Guzzo, R. A., & Dickson, M. W. (1996). Teams in organizations: recent research on performance and effectiveness. *Annual Review Of Psychology,* 307-338. DOI: 10.1146/annurev.psych.47.1.307.

Halford, S., & Savage, M. (2010). Reconceptualizing digital social inequality. *Information, Communication & Society,* 13(7), 937-955. DOI: 10.1080/1369118X.2010.499956.

Hall, E. T. (1976). *Beyond culture.* Garden City, N.Y.: Anchor Press, 1976.

Hall, E.T. (1983). *The dance of life.* Garden City, NY: Anchor Press/Doubleday.

Hamada, B. (2004). ICTs and cultural diversity with special reference to the Islamic perspective. *Journal of International Communication,* 10(1), 34. DOI: 10.1080/13216597.2004.9751963.

Hampton, K. N., Lee, C., & Her, E. (2011). How new media affords network diversity: Direct and mediated access to social capital through participation in local social settings. *New Media & Society,* 13(7), 1031-1049. DOI: 10.1177/1461444810390342.

Hofstede, G. H. (1991). *Cultures and organizations: Software of the mind.* London,UK: McGraw-Hill.

Hoter, E., Shonfeld, M., & Ganayim, A. (2009). Information and communication technology (ICT) in the service of multiculturalism. *International Review of Research in Open and Distance Learning,* 10(2).

Hsin Hsin, C., Shuang-Shii, C., & Shu Han, C. (2011). Determinants of cultural adaptation, communication quality, and trust in virtual teams' performance. *Total Quality Management & Business Excellence,* 22(3), 305-329. DOI: 10.1080/14783363.2010.532319.

Hung, Y.-T. C., & Nguyen, M. T. T. D. (2008). The impact of cultural diversity on global virtual team collaboration: A social identity perspective. *Proceedings of the 41st Annual Hawaii International Conference on System Sciences (HICSS 2008)* (pp. 1-10). Washington DC: IEEE. DOI: 10.1109/HICSS.2008.441.

James, J. (2011). Are changes in the digital divide consistent with global equality or inequality?. *Information Society,* 27(2), 121-128. DOI: 10.1080/01972243.2011.548705.

Jarvenpaa, S. L., & Liedner, D. E. (1999). Communication and trust in global virtual teams. *Organization Science,* 10(6), 791-815. DOI: 10.1287/orsc.10.6.791.

Kamwendo, G. H. (2008). Globalization, linguistic diversity, and information dissemination in Malawi. *Perspectives on Global Development & Technology,* 7(3/4), 271-280. DOI: 10.1163/156914908X370700.

Kayan, S., Fussell, S. R., & Setlock, L. D. (2006). Cultural differences in the use of instant messaging in Asia and North America. *Proc. CSCW* 2006.

Kaye, G., & Little, S. (2000). Dysfunctional development pathways of information and communication technology: Cultural conflicts. *Journal of Global Information Management,* 8(1), 5. DOI: 10.4018/jgim.2000010101.

Kayworth, T. R., Leidner, D. E. (2001). Leadership effectiveness in global virtual teams. *Journal of Management Information Systems*, 18(3), 7-40.

Kling, R. (1998). A brief introduction to social informatics. *Canadian Journal of Information and Library Science - Revue Canadienne des Sciences de l'Information et de Bibliotheconomie*, 23(1-2), 50-85.

Kling, R. (1999). What is social informatics and why does it matter?. *D-Lib Magazine* 5, no. 1: Library, Information Science & Technology Abstracts, EBSCOhost. DOI: 10.1045/january99-kling.

Kluckhohn, C., Strodbeck, F. L. (1961). *Variation in value orientation*. Evanson, IL: Row and Peterson.

Komito, L. (2011). Social media and migration: Virtual community 2.0. *Journal of the American Society for Information Science and Technology*, 62, 1075–1086. DOI: 10.1002/asi.21517.

Lauring, J., & Klitmøller, A. (2010). Communicating in multicultural firms: Boundary creation, fragmentation and the social use of ICT. In: *Organizational communication and sustainable development: ICTs for mobility* (pp. 135-152). Hershey, PA: Information Science Reference/IGI. DOI: 10.4018/978-1-4666-1601-1.ch050.

Lee, O. (2002). Cultural differences in e-mail use of virtual teams: A critical social theory perspective. *Cyberpsychology & Behavior*, 5(3), 227-232. DOI: 10.1089/109493102760147222.

Leidner, D. E., & Kayworth, T. (2006). Review: A review of culture in information systems research: Toward a theory of information technology culture conflict. *MIS Quarterly*, 30(2), 357-399.

Lievrouw, L. A. (1998). Our own devices: Heterotopic communication, discourse, and culture in the information society, *The Information Society: An International Journal*, 14:2, 83-96. DOI:10.1080/019722498128890.

Lisak, A., & Erez, M. (2009). Leaders and followers in multi-cultural teams: Their effects on team communication, team identity and team effectiveness.

In Fussell, S. et al (Ed.), *Proceedings of the 2009 International Workshop on Intercultural Collaboration* (pp. 81-88). New York, NY: ACM. DOI: 10.1145/1499224.1499238.

Luo, A., & Olson, J. S. (2008). How collaboratories affect scientists from developing countries. In G. M. Olson, A. Zimmerman, & N. Bos (Eds.), *Scientific Collaboration on the Internet* (pp.365-376). Cambridge, Mass.: MIT Press. DOI: 10.7551/mitpress/9780262151207.003.0021.

Luukkonen, T., Persson, O., & Sivertson, G. (1992). Understanding patterns of international scientific collaboration. *Science, Technology, & Human Values*, 17(1), 101-126. DOI: 10.1177/016224399201700106.

Mahdjoubi, L., & Moobela, C. (2008). Unlocking the barriers to participation of black and minority ethnic communities in the decision-making processes: The potential of multimedia. *International Journal Of Diversity In Organisations, Communities & Nations*, 8(2), 141.

Massey, A., Hung, Y.-T. C., Montoya-Weiss, M., & Ramesh, V. (2001). When culture and style aren't about clothes: Perceptions of task-technology "fit" in global virtual teams. *Proceedings of GROUP 2001* (pp. 207-213). DOI: 10.1145/500286.500318.

Mayers, M. D., & Tan, F. B. (2002). Beyond models of national culture in information systems research. *Journal of Global Information Systems*, 10(1), 24-32. DOI: 10.4018/jgim.2002010103.

Mikawa, S. P., Cunnington, S. K., & Gaskins, S. A. (2009). Removing barriers to trust in distributed teams: Understanding cultural differences and strengthening social ties. In Fussell, S. et al (Ed.), *Proceedings of the 2009 International Workshop on Intercultural Collaboration* (pp. 273-276). New York, NY: ACM. DOI: 10.1145/1499224.1499275.

Monaka, K. C., & Mutula, S. M. (2010). An inclusive linguistic framework for Botswana: Reconciling the state and perceived marginalized communities. *Journal of Information, Information Technology & Organizations*, 5, 51-65.

Montoya-Weiss, M. M., Massey, A. P., & Song, M. (2001). Getting it together: temporal coordination and conflict management in global virtual teams. *Academy of Management Journal*, 44 (6), 1251-1262. DOI: 10.2307/3069399.

Mutula, S. M. (2005). Peculiarities of the digital divide in Sub-Saharan Africa. *Program: Electronic Library and Information Systems*, 39(2), 122-138. DOI: 10.1108/00330330510595706.

Naor, M., Liderman, K., & Schroeder, R. (2010). The globalization of operations in Eastern and Western countries: Unpacking the relationship between national and organizational culture and its impact on manufacturing performance. *Journal of Operations Management*, 28, 194-205. DOI: 10.1016/j.jom.2009.11.001.

Niederman, F., & Tan, F. B. (2011). Emerging markets managing global IT teams: Considering cultural dynamics. Communications of The ACM, 54(4), 24-27. DOI: 10.1145/1924421.1924431.

Nurmi, N., Bosch-Sijtsema, P., Sivunen, A., & Fruchter, R. (2009). Who shouts louder? Exerting power across distance and culture. In Fussell, S. et al (Eds.), *Proceedings of the 2009 International Workshop on Intercultural Collaboration* (pp. 71-80). New York, NY: ACM. DOI: 10.1145/1499224.1499237.

Oetzel, J.G. (2001). Self-construals, communication processes, and group outcomes in homogeneous and heterogeneous groups. *Small Group Research*, 32(1), 19-54. DOI: 10.1177/104649640103200102.

Olson, J. S. & Olson, G. M. (2003-2004). Culture surprises in remote software development teams. *ACM: Queue*, 1(9), 52-59. DOI: 10.1145/966789.966804.

Oyedemi, T. (2009). Social inequalities and the South African ICT access policy agendas. *International Journal of Communication*, 3, 151-168.

Palaiologou, N. (2009). Needs for developing culturally oriented supportive learning with the aid of information and communication technologies. *Pedagogy, Culture and Society*, 17(2), 189-200. DOI: 10.1080/14681360902934434.

Papaioannou, T. (2011). Technological innovation, global justice and politics of development. *Progress in Development Studies*, 11(4), 321-338. DOI: 10.1177/146499341001100404.

Pauleen, D. J., & Yoong, P. (2001). Relationship building and the use of ICT in boundary-crossing virtual teams: a facilitator's perspective. *Journal of Information Technology* (Routledge, Ltd.), 16(4), 205. DOI: 10.1080/02683960110100391.

Pfeffer, J., and H. Leblebici (1977). Information technology and organizational structure. *The Pacific Sociological Review*, 20(2), 241-261. DOI: 10.2307/1388934.

Purwanto, S. A. (2011). Information & communication technology (ICT) and the challenge of multicultural society: Some cases of internet-facilitated interaction in Indonesia. *OMNES: The Journal of Multicultural Society*, 2(2), 1-21.

Quinones, P. A., Fussell, S. R., Soibelman, L., & Akinci, B. (2009). Bridging the gap: Discovering mental models in globally collaborative contexts. In Fussell, S. et al (Ed.), *Proceedings of the 2009 International Workshop on Intercultural Collaboration* (pp. 101-110). New York, NY: ACM. DOI: 10.1145/1499224.1499241.

Relly, J. E., & Cuillier, D. (2010). A comparison of political, cultural, and economic indicators of access to information in Arab and non-Arab states, *Government Information Quarterly*, 27(4), 360-370, ISSN 0740-624X, 10.1016/j.giq.2010.04.004. Retrieved from http://www.sciencedirect.com/science/article/pii/S0740624X10000626.

Rob Kling Center for Social Informatics. (2013). About social informatics. Retrieved from: http://rkcsi.indiana.edu/socialinformatics.html.

Saleh, I. (2011). ICT contours in Africa's development: Prospects and concerns. Conference Papers — International Communication Association, 1-32.

Sanfilippo, M., & Fichman, P. (forthcoming). Social Informatics: Milestones, opportunities and challenges. In P. Fichman & H. Rosenbaum (Eds). *Social Informatics: Past, Present and Future*. Cambridge Scholars Publishing.

Sassi, S. (2005). Cultural differentiation or social segregation? Four approaches to the digital divide. *New Media & Society*, 7(5), 684-700. DOI: 10.1177/1461444805056012.

Schadewitz, N., & Zakaria, N. (2009). Cross-cultural collaboration Wiki: Evolving knowledge about international teamwork. In Fussell, S. et al (Ed.), *Proceedings of the 2009 International Workshop on Intercultural Collaboration* (pp. 301-304). New York, NY: ACM. DOI: 10.1145/1499224.1499282.

Schein, E. H. (1992). *Organizational culture and leadership*. (2nd ed.) San Francisco, CA: Jossey-Bass.

Setlock, L. D., Fussell, S. R., Ji, E., & Culver, M. (2009). Sorry to interrupt: Asian media preferences in cross-cultural collaborations. In Fussell, S. et al (Ed.), *Proceedings of the 2009 International Workshop on Intercultural Collaboration* (pp. 309-312). New York, NY: ACM. DOI: 10.1145/1499224.1499284.

Setlock, L. D., Fussell, S. R., & Neuwirth, C. (2004). Taking it out of context: Collaborating within and across cultures in face-to-face settings and via instant messaging. *Proceedings of CSCW 2004* (pp. 604-613). DOI: 10.1145/1031607.1031712.

Setlock, L. D., Quinones, P. A., & Fussell, S. R. (2007). Does culture interact with media richness? The effects of audio vs. video conferencing on Chinese and American dyads. *Proceedings of HICSS* 2007.

Shachaf, P. (2005). Bridging cultural diversity through email. *Journal of Global Information Technology Management*, 8(2), 46-60.

Shachaf, P. (2008). Cultural diversity and information and communication technology impacts on global virtual teams: An exploratory study. *Information & Management*, 45(2), 131-142. DOI: 10.1016/j.im.2007.12.003.

Shachaf, P., & Hara, N. (2005). Team effectiveness in virtual environments: An ecological approach. In P. Ferris & S. Godar (Eds.), *Teaching and learning with virtual teams* (pp. 83-108). Hershey, PA: Idea Group Publishing, Inc. DOI: 10.4018/978-1-59140-708-9.ch004.

Shachaf, P., & Hara, N. (2007). Behavioral complexity theory of media selection: A proposed theory for global virtual teams. *Journal of Information Science*, 33(1), 63-75. DOI: 10.1177/0165551506068145.

Shokef, E. & Erez, M. (2006). Global work culture and global identity, as a platform for a shared understanding in multicultural teams/Shared meaning systems in multicultural teams. In B. Mannix, Neale, M., & Chen, Ya-Ru (Eds.). *National culture and groups*. Research on Managing Groups and Teams, 9, pp. 325-352. Elsevier JAI Press: San Diego: CA. DOI: 10.1016/S1534-0856(06)09013-X.

Siakas, K. V. (2008). A distributed multicultural network for teaching information society: Cultural diversity aspects. *Proceedings of the 6th International Conference on Networked Learning*, 774-782.

Sieck, W. R. & Mueller, S. T. (2009). Cultural variations in collaborative decision making: Driven by beliefs or social norms? In Fussell, S. et al (Ed.), *Proceedings of the 2009 International Workshop on Intercultural Collaboration* (pp. 111-118). New York, NY: ACM. DOI: 10.1145/1499224.1499242.

Srinivasan, R. (2013). Bridges between cultural and digital worlds in revolutionary Egypt, *The Information Society: An International Journal*, 29:1, 49-60. DOI: 10.1080/01972243.2012.739594.

Straub, D., Loch, K., Evaristo, R., Karahanna, E., & Srite, M. (2002). Toward a theory-based measurement of culture. *Journal of Global Information Management*, 10(1), 13-23. DOI: 10.4018/jgim.2002010102.

Takahashi, C., Yamagishi, T., Liu, J. H., Wang, F., Lin, Y., & Yu, S. (2008). The intercultural trust paradigm: Studying joint cultural interaction and social exchange in real time over the Internet. *International Journal of Intercultural Relations*, 32, 215-228. DOI: 10.1016/j.ijintrel.2007.11.003.

Trompenaars, F., & Hampden-Turner. C. (1998). *Riding the waves of culture: Understanding cultural diversity in global business.* New York: McGraw-Hill.

Wang, H.-C., Fussell, S. R., & Setlock, L. D. (2009). Cultural difference and adaptation of communication styles in computer-mediated group brainstorming. Cross culture CMC, *Proceedings of AMC CHI 2009 Conference on Human Factors in Computng Systems* (pp. 669-678). New York, NY: AMC. DOI: 10.1145/1518701.1518806.

Zheng, Y., & Walsham, G. (2008). Inequality of what? Social exclusion in the e-society as capability deprivation. *Information Technology & People*, 21(3), 222-243. DOI: 10.1108/09593840810896000.

Author Biographies

Pnina Fichman is an Associate Professor in the School of Informatics and Computing and the Director of the Rob Kling Center of Social Informatics. Her research in social informatics focuses on the relationships between information technologies and cultural diversity, and the consequences and impacts of this interaction on group process and outcomes. She studies processes and outcomes of crowds, online communities, virtual teams, and information intermediation. In addition, her research addresses motivation for, perception of, and reaction to online deviant behaviors, such as trolling and discrimination. She has published articles in such publications as *Information and Management*, *Journal of the American Society for Information Science & Technology*, and *Journal of Information Science*. She earned her Ph.D. from SILS UNC in 2003.

Madelyn Sanfilippo is a second-year doctoral student in Information Science at Indiana University, Bloomington's School of Informatics and Computing. Madelyn is interested in the relationship between social inequality and information inequality. Her work addresses social and political issues surrounding information and information technology access. She plans to specifically consider the interaction between information policy and information technology in the domain of government information, from a social informatics perspective, in her doctoral research.

Printed in the United States
by Baker & Taylor Publisher Services